Prosperity
AFTER DIVORCE

How to take charge of your finances &
create the life you really want using
LIFESTYLE RE-DESIGN PLANNING™

MICHELL

D1445532

PROSPERITY PRESS
Fueling Financial Knowledge & Growth

Prosperity Press
c/o Jacobik Enterprises, LLC
P.O. Box 171
Taftville, CT 06380

ISBN-13: 978-0-692-04975-4

Editor: Bryna Haynes, TheHeartofWriting.com
Interior layout and design: Bryna Haynes, TheHeartofWriting.com
Cover design: Bryna Haynes, TheHeartofWriting.com
Cover Photo: Lev via AdobeStock (Image #59753364)
Author Photo: J. Fiereck Photography

Prosperity After Divorce™ and LifeStyle Re-Design Planning™ are trademarks of Michelle Jacobik

Dedication

To Amanda and Alex, with all my love.

Praise

"With wit, humor, and a bit of (enlightened) tough love, Michelle Jacobik navigates you through your post-divorce financial journey. *Prosperity After Divorce* gives you the tools you need to create a solid framework for a financial life on your own—including that big, bad B-word: budget! You'll laugh, you'll cry … and then you'll get to work."

- **Barbara Stanny** (now Barbara Huson), author of *Sacred Success* and *Secrets of Six-Figure Women*

"Michelle Jacobik has been a contributor to *DivorceForce*. Here, in *Prosperity After Divorce*, she provides all the wisdom and help we have come to know. While Michelle teaches us about financial prosperity, she also goes much deeper and provides a 'LifeStyle Re-Design Plan.' What exactly is life prosperity? Read, find out, get on board, and start your new fulfilled life."

- *DivorceForce Magazine*

Table of Contents

—◆◈◆—

PART II: DESIGN THE LIFE YOU WANT

PART III: THE GRAND RE-DESIGN

PART IV: WORKSHEETS

EXTRAS

Prosperity

AFTER DIVORCE

Introduction

THE TREES

As a child, I came to life while swinging on a tire swing tied to a branch, or scurrying up a tree trunk like a squirrel. I tested, almost methodically, which branches were weak, which were strong, and which would bend but not break under my weight. Inevitably, I found a crook between trunk and branch to cuddle into for a few hours.

The view from the top gave me a different perspective. I could see things that were invisible from the ground. Everything seemed more expansive, and at the same time more accessible.

When I became a woman, trees were a constant symbol of wisdom and strength for me. Shortly after my divorce in 2009, I booked a weekend self-care retreat at the Kripalu Center in the Berkshires in Massachusetts. The grounds are surrounded by the most amazing, ancient trees, and crisscrossed with peaceful hiking paths.

One afternoon, I spread a blanket under the canopy of a hundred-year-old maple, and pulled out my journal. "What is coming next for me?" I asked. My whole world had been uprooted by my divorce, and I wanted Divine reassurance that everything was going to be okay.

As the words poured onto the pages, my writing shifted from addressing my question to reflecting on the trees around me. The tree under which I sat, and its brothers and sisters in the forest, knew their purpose. They were rooted in their own knowing, and they grew strong despite all the adversity they had to weather. Despite wind, rain, and winter storms, they stood tall and strong, and they thrived.

Under this magnificent tree, I could feel my strength. Just as it did, I could weather the storms of my life, and emerge taller and stronger than ever before. I just had to dig deep, find my roots, and give myself the nourishment I needed to keep growing.

The last line of my journal entry for that day was, *In the strength of your roots, I find my strength. In the presence of your knowing, I find my knowing.*

Ever since that day, when I have felt like life's storms were too much for me to withstand, I remember that maple tree, and I feel comforted.

"Okay, Michelle," you may be saying. "That's great (and maybe a little woo-woo)—but what the heck do trees have to do with prosperity after divorce?"

Well, here's the thing. We are all like the trees. When our roots go deep, and our trunks are strong, we can withstand anything. We prosper, no matter what life throws at us. But when our foundation is weak, or we ignore the things that are eating at our stability and prosperity (like our unconscious money habits, emotional spending, or unhelpful beliefs), we are much more likely to crash.

The great news is, you don't have to seek your prosperity alone. Have you ever seen the stakes they set up around infant trees in the city parks? Those structures of wood and wire provide support and stability for the trees until they grow strong enough to stand on their own. This book is like the support system for your blossoming tree, with the six pillars of my LifeStyle Re-Design Planning process functioning as the stakes, and your effort and intention serving as the ties. Even if you feel like a leaning tree right now, on the verge of toppling, you will find everything you need on these pages to reorient yourself, get grounded, and reach for the sky.

****

I have to be honest: I never thought I would write a book.

For several years now, I've been helping women thrive after divorce by organizing and systemizing their finances, and creating goals that move them toward their version of prosperity. Money is my genius zone. I'm a numbers whiz; nothing makes me happier than a functional budget and a mathematically-sound plan. I deal in reality, not in wishes. I look at what is, not what could or "should" be. This means that I'm able to achieve real results for people in real life. I get change out of people's heads on onto their balance sheets.

But here's the thing I've noticed: money alone doesn't equal prosperity. Even when the numbers line up, if we don't *feel* prosperous, secure, and supported within ourselves, all the money in the world won't solve our problems. We become like uprooted trees, just waiting for the axe to fall.

Working with dozens of clients over a period of a few years, I began to notice consistent patterns. Women came to me to help them understand their finances, but as we delved into their money habits, beliefs, and fears, we encountered prosperity blocks that had nothing to do with dollars and cents. Sometimes these blocks were directly related to their divorce situations, but often they were lifelong patterns that were triggered in new ways by the upheaval in their lives. By "staking their trees" in six key areas—Finances, Emotions, Habits, Work, Family, and Spirituality—we were able to address their deep-seated issues and create solid ground for them to replant their roots and grow stronger.

Yes. By mapping out their budgets and examining their financial habits, my clients and I were able to tap into their deepest dreams, desires, and visions, and release unhelpful patterns and behaviors that had been plaguing them for years, even decades.

It was nothing short of a revelation for me. I mean, I'm a budget coach, not a therapist! And yet, to this day, every time I sit down with a woman to map out her plan for prosperity after divorce, we end up shifting something deeper and more profound than her bank account balance.

The more stories I heard from clients, the more I felt compelled to share this work with a wider audience—but it wasn't until early 2017 that I got the nudge from my Higher Power to turn my LifeStyle Re-Design Planning program into a book. (Actually, it was more than a nudge. It was a shove!) You hold in your hands the fruit of that Universal prompting.

My wish for you is that you not only heal from your divorce (or whatever life storms have brought you to this place), but that you find true prosperity—that you send your roots deep into your inner knowing, your branches higher than your wildest dreams, and your leaves questing for the sun and all the brilliance life can offer.

HOW TO USE THIS BOOK

This book is a combination of story, narrative exploration, and practical exercises. I've endeavored to take what would normally be considered a "dry" subject and make it fun and relatable (and I owe a tremendous debt of gratitude to my clients who generously shared their stories). I hope you cry, giggle, and grin while reading it as much as I did while writing it!

In Part I, we'll learn why money is the gateway to creating real, lasting change in your life—but not the sole ingredient in prosperity. We'll talk about some of the reasons why divorce triggers our money and security issues, and how we can address these concerns in a holistic way.

In Part II, we'll explore the six Pillars of the LifeStyle Re-Design Planning process, tackle the big, bad B-word (your budget), and go through some practical exercises to get an accurate picture of where you are right now (no BS or wishes!) so you can actually make a plan to get to where you want to go.

In Part III, we'll put it all together into your LifeStyle Re-Design Plan—the dynamic growth plan you will use to create, step by step, your prosperity after divorce.

Throughout the book, we're going to go deep and get real. We're going to talk about things you had no idea had anything to do with money—like your family life, spirituality, and emotional habits. We're going to pull back all the curtains and see what's actually going on for you, so you can put your inner wisdom and outer resources to work to clear away anything that no longer serves you.

Your prosperity journey starts here.

Are you ready to root down?

Part I

WHAT IS PROSPERITY,
ANYWAY?

Chapter One

LIFE, RE-DESIGNED

It was the evening of my fifteenth wedding anniversary, and as usual we had made plans to have dinner out at a fancy restaurant. I wanted to celebrate, because we had *done it*, dammit! We had made it for a decade and a half—through challenge after challenge, thick and thin, sickness and health.

I dressed like I was preparing to attend the Academy Awards. It didn't matter that we had been pissed off and cold to one another for the past two weeks; tonight, we would put all of that aside to celebrate this huge milestone.

The car ride to the restaurant was filled with the "normals." We talked about what the kids had done that day, how things were going for me at work, our plans for the weekend. Once there, our food came out quickly, and we spent more time savoring the delicious meal than talking.

We ended the celebration with nightcaps of Sambuca and Baileys and got back in the car.

Silence. Just dead, awful silence. The celebration was over, and we were right back to where we'd been for weeks. Or months. Or maybe years. The air felt so stale that I had to open a window.

What had we been celebrating? I wondered. A thriving partnership, or just our ability to keep playing the parts we knew so well? Had I just ended, with a toast, the biggest performance of my life?

Neither of us said a word the whole ride home. The moment we were out of the car, he made some excuse about wanting to watch the game. I stepped out of my flashy heels and headed upstairs to bed, even more desolate than I had been before.

Our life looked pretty amazing from the outside. Two incredible kids, one boy and one girl. A gorgeous house on a cul-de-sac with a two-bay garage and a big pool. Two cars, a truck, and a fertilized lawn. We had everything most people dream of, and more.

And yet, we weren't happy. We were two adults who were great at parenting but lousy at loving each other. Our walls were getting higher by the day; neither of us could accept where the other was at. I was numbing with work and ambition; he was numbing with booze and drugs. Our paths weren't parallel. They weren't even heading in the same general direction.

We'd been battling this division for longer than I cared to remember. I'd spent the last five years working on myself— reading the books, taking up yoga, and leaning on friends who weren't afraid to tell me where I needed to make improvements. I listened to self-help podcasts on the way to and from work. I joined the PTO (only to find out that I wasn't the only parent in the world who wasn't at those meetings). I recited the Serenity Prayer multiple times a day, and sent "blessings" to my husband, hoping he would feel them and stop acting like a self-destructive teenager. I even signed us up for marriage counseling on more than one occasion.

Nothing worked. Fighting the rift only seemed to make it deeper. It was like we were living on a fault line, waiting for the monster quake to finally swallow us up.

On a morning, not too long after that awful anniversary, I woke up with one thought ringing in my head: "This is *not* the life I want!"

Half of my soul—the half that I'd entrusted to my partner—was dying. Maybe it was already dead. And if I didn't make a change, the other half was going to die, too.

I went through my "wants and needs list"—the tally I'd been keeping in my head for months. If you're a woman reading this, you know exactly what I mean. My needs were simple: a partner who was a loving father, who didn't abuse me or cheat on me, and who would be steady and reliable when I needed support. My wants were less easy to define: a partner who was spiritual, who valued friendship and family the way I do, who was willing to be open to change and growth, and who woke up each day feeling grateful for the life we created. I wanted someone who didn't turn to drugs and alcohol every time he had a bad day, who loved vacationing, and who got excited about life beyond the latest football match or boxing showcase.

My husband was meeting my *needs* about 80 percent of the time, and there was no doubt that he was a great father. But my *wants* were not even on his radar. Even to me, they seemed unrealistic, needy, selfish. My heart's desires were getting dusty; the ink was fading—until that morning, when I woke up knowing, with total certainty, that my wants and my needs were actually the same. I just had to be strong enough to step forward and make a change.

THE NOT-SO-BIG ANNOUNCEMENT

You'd think that, upon having this massive realization, the first thing I'd do would be to tell someone—you know, like my best friend, or my mom. Nope. Instead, I got dressed, dropped the kids at their respective schools, and headed off to run my business like it was an ordinary day.

I didn't cry. No one asked me what was wrong. I just plowed through my to-do list like usual—until I stepped into our employee kitchen to make a cup of coffee, and caught sight of a magnet on the refrigerator. On it was the number for our Employee Assistance Program, a service designed to help employees resolve their personal problems. I carried the magnet back to my desk, shut the door, and dialed the number.

"Can I help you?" the operator chimed.

I explained that I was one of the owners of the business providing this benefit package.

"Do you need to speak to someone in billing?" she asked.

"No, I need some information about how to access counseling for myself."

"Oh! Well, let me see … It looks like Bob has an opening at one o'clock. Will that work for you?"

I closed my eyes and took a deep breath. "Yes. I'll be there."

On the ride to that appointment, I wondered how I was going to tell a complete stranger the story of my marriage—and its breakdown—in fifty minutes. I thought, *Maybe I'll get lucky and this guy won't have a two o'clock. Then I'll have the time to explain how I feel and get what I need out of this session.*

But then, another thought appeared, in no uncertain terms: *The story doesn't matter. Just ask for what you want and need.*

"Okay," I asked aloud. "What do I need?"

I needed someone who could hold me accountable, who would make sure I didn't change my mind this time out of fear. I needed someone who could walk me through the process of dissolving a fifteen-year marriage, and support me and my kids through the earthquake that was about to rock our world.

And the person I'd chosen for this role? A random therapist named Bob.

Poor Bob.

****

The session actually went better than I expected. Bob was great. Once we got through the initial meet-and-greet stuff, we talked about my biggest reservation around leaving my marriage: the breaking of my vow. I was raised Catholic, and I had pledged myself to my husband in front of God and 125 of my closest family and friends. I took that vow seriously. How would God ever forgive me for breaking it? I mean, my parents weren't always happy. My grandparents weren't always happy. Shouldn't I just ride with the status quo and keep up the performance for another decade or three, until we were too old to start over anyway?

Bob never dismissed my vow attachment. In fact, he gave me the conviction I needed to move forward by asking me to write new vows—this time to myself.

"But I'm still breaking the big one—the God one!" I lamented. "How will this help?"

"Just try it," he said.

At the end of the session, Bob handed me a handmade paper

journal made in Bali. It was "crunchy-feely," a unique treasure.

"Write," he told me.

It was as if he'd just handed me a permission slip to create my own *Eat, Pray, Love*-style story of self-reinvention entitled *My New Life*. I was so grateful I almost hugged him. It was empowering to know that, despite the process feeling so random, I had chosen the right person to support me.

That night, I opened the journal, and stared at that first blank page. Where should I start? What vows could I make to myself that would be as meaningful as the ones I'd made to my partner?

I took a breath, and wrote, "I, Michelle, take *you* for better or worse, for richer or poorer, in sickness and in health. I promise to love, cherish, honor, and protect you for all the days of your life."

I read it again, and wept. All of the books, seminars, articles, and meditation I had listened to about self-care, self-acceptance, and self-worth over the years ... they all clicked in that moment. Bob was right: I needed to commit to a new vow and see this life change in a new light. I hadn't stopped loving or honoring my spouse. I just needed to do it from a distance in order to love *me* again.

A NEW MANTRA

As the proud co-owner of a women-owned, women-operated business, I thought I had seen it all. I'd employed more than twenty-five women in fifteen years, and seen them through every stage of life. I'd stood beside women who were fighting cancer; one won the battle, one did not. I'd stood beside sleep-deprived new moms as they sobbed out their anxiety, and older moms attending court dates for kids who'd made bad decisions. I'd stood beside women struggling to support their spouses through depression, gambling addictions, drug use, alcoholism, and job losses.

Through all these bumps in the road of life, I tried to provide a place of safety, security, and support. I coached my employees to use their office day as a means to leave the hard stuff behind for a while. "Breathe here," I'd say, "and you can pick up your stuff again at the door." (In the earliest years, that probably sounded more like, "Check your shit at the door and do your job!" But the more I saw "real life" show up for me and other people, the more I understood that this advice wasn't as easy as I thought.)

And now, here I was, struggling with my own mantra. My safe haven—my office—no longer felt safe. I couldn't check my shit at the door. I couldn't even keep my shit under my hat. Every day, I felt like my decision to divorce was affecting my life more and more. I couldn't focus. I would start a task, and five minutes later find myself unsure of what I was doing. I would hear a song playing on the office surround sound system, and suddenly I'd be awash with emotion. There were stretches when I couldn't recall when I had last eaten, or what I'd done the day before. I misplaced files, keys, and even my car in a parking lot.

For weeks, I didn't tell anyone except my business partner and two closest counterparts about what was happening, but I wondered if everyone could see right through me as I trudged along, trying to act normal.

When I finally did start telling people, my tendency was just to come out and say it. "I'm getting a divorce." But even as I mouthed the words, I don't think I truly absorbed what was about to happen. I felt like there was a glass wall between me and my feelings. I knew I was sad, but I couldn't explain "sad." I couldn't cry at night, even though we were now sleeping separately.

Honestly, I wanted to fast-forward through this part of the process. I wanted everything to be over, so I could get on with my new life—but it was like every day lasted eighty hours.

"What is going on?" I asked Bob in one session. "I friggin' *wanted* this!"

"You're grieving," Bob said gently. "And you're avoiding your grief. You wanted to walk through this, not around it."

"I didn't know it would be this hard."

"Yes, well, grief is hard. But it's also necessary. You will get through this."

Grief finally came in the form of tears, negative thoughts, exhaustion, and lethargy. I moved at half-speed, and was just … quiet. A lot. (That, for me, is just *not* normal.) Thank God I had someone who could explain to me that I wasn't on the verge of a nervous breakdown or some pre-menopausal explosion. Once I understood that this was how grief looked, for me, I was able to accept it.

And that was when I realized that divorce didn't just mean changing my Facebook relationship status and finding a fun new apartment. I was about to restructure my *whole life*. I was leaving my husband of fifteen years—my late-teen soulmate—and releasing him to grow and live *without me*.

I read somewhere that divorce has been called "death without a body." It certainly felt that way at first. But, as Bob reminded me, in every season, something must die in order for something new to be born. I held on to that thought daily, and gave myself permission to be in this current season without apology. I allowed myself to truly believe that, if I turned off the guilt tapes that were playing in my mind, got the support I needed, and took care of my mind and body, that new season would come, and my new "self" would show up to live this new life.

That's the thing about divorce. When we step out of that old relationship, we also step out of our old selves—our old beliefs, habits, patterns, standards, and judgments—and that can be incredibly challenging. In order to give ourselves an anchor in the storm, we need to choose a new focus—a new mantra to live by.

Unless I wanted to be a major hypocrite, my mantra could no longer be "check your shit at the door." I needed to choose a new focus. I chose "prosperity."

Prosperity. I love that word. It feels … full. Fulfilling. I love the idea of "prospering," of being "prosperous."

But what does *prosperity* actually mean?

WHAT IS PROSPERITY, ANYWAY?

If you had asked me five years pre-divorce, I would have said that "prosperity" was having lots of money, and living the "good life."

My business was successful. Like, *really* successful. We had grown to over $12 million in sales. I had money coming out my ears. My house was magazine-gorgeous. My kids got everything they wanted and more. We took elaborate vacations to amazing destinations, and I never hesitated to whip out my credit card to indulge a whim.

But, as you already know, it was all a shell. Except for my relationships with my kids, it was empty. I had money, but I didn't have prosperity.

You see, prosperity, as I now define it, is about having the space to thrive. It means having those needs and wants met—

not just in terms of material things, but in terms of feeling worthy, supported, and confident. Prosperity is about living life on your own terms, according to your own rules. It's about not pretending anymore, even when the truth is butt-ugly and has teeth like sabers.

I had money before my divorce, but it was only afterward—when the money, the dream house, and the picture-perfect fantasy were gone—that I found *real* prosperity and contentment.

The Bottom Line

In this book, I'm going to share how I, and several of my clients, found that place where wants and needs meet in the real world, redesigned our lives, and found true prosperity after divorce. No matter where you are right now, I know this book will help you to see your path forward.

As you progress through this book, you'll see that everything I teach is viewed through the lens of finance. After all, I'm a financial coach. This may seem strange, considering what I just shared about prosperity and money being two different entities. But here's the thing: money is a perfect gateway to designing and understanding your new life. In divorce, money is our biggest stressor. It's our survival. It's our lifeline. And how we use it, manage it, and relate to it can mean the difference between a new life on our own terms and a life lived at someone else's direction.

The seasons are turning. Change is coming. You have permission to step into your new life, and make a new vow to honor, cherish, love, and support *you*—for richer and poorer, in sickness and in health, 'til death do you part.

Are you ready to take the leap?

Chapter Two

IF MARRIAGE IS ABOUT LOVE, HAPPINESS, AND SECURITY, WHAT IS DIVORCE ABOUT?

When we get married for the first time, it's all about love. Our expectation, as we enter into this sacred union, is that we and our beloved will be inseparable in all areas, from now until death do us part. We spend months looking for the perfect setting, the perfect colors, the perfect décor and *hors d'oeuvres*. We spend hours listening to songs, looking for the perfect tune to capture our eternal devotion and the way we want our lives to play out from our wedding day forward.

My wedding song was "Music Box" by Mariah Carey. The lyrics seemed to capture the essence of our commitment to one another. We would spend our years "chasing away each other's fears" and helping each other find "brighter places" in the rat race of life. With love on our side, we would get through it all.

There were no lines in that song about broken communication. No lines about past hurts. No lines about walls so tall we couldn't see over them. No lines about First Named Plaintiff versus First Named Defendant. When I reread those lyrics I had put so much care into choosing, I wondered what it would have taken to create that fairy-tale ending. Even through the perfect lens of hindsight, I still can't see the answer clearly.

What I do know is that the security I wanted from my partner on November 26, 1994—my wedding day—was not the same security I wanted when I walked out of the courtroom on October 8, 2009. It was no longer about *him* lifting me up, or chasing away my fears. Now, I had to do those things for myself.

The issue was that I had no idea how to create my own sense of security. I'd always believed, naively, that security was sort of a given in marriage, something each partner did for the other, but that turned out to be a farce. How could I position myself and my kids to be free from fear? How could I reduce the anxiety that my kids and I were feeling?

As I reached for the door handle, hands shaking, and slid into my car to drive away from the courthouse, I felt broken. My emotional, physical, and financial stability all felt challenged. But I'd made my choice—the right choice for me—and there was no going back.

Nothing could have prepared me for the shakeup that was to come. Alimony, child support, expenses for a home I was no longer living in, "startup" costs and a security deposit for my newly-rented house: when all was said and done, my once-substantial income was stretched to the limit. Plus, I had to pay out giant chunks of my savings, retirement accounts, and investments. For the first time since my early twenties, I was worried about going broke.

I'd said I wanted prosperity; what I got felt like anything but.

Was this some kind of cruel joke? Was the Universe laughing at me for thinking I could have it all?

Yes, marriage is about love. But divorce is about *money*.

WHY MONEY AND DIVORCE ARE INSEPARABLE

Once I started working with my new mantra, "Prosperity After Divorce," discovering the keys to prosperity became my all-consuming focus. I wanted prosperity. I *craved* it. When I found it, it would mean that the divorce was behind me—that I'd healed, that I'd arrived in a new place, and that all the heartache, loss, and grief was finally over for good.

Now that I knew what I wanted, I needed to access my own definition of prosperity and create a life around it. I knew, deep down, that prosperity wasn't just about having lots of cash—but once my divorce process started, it seemed like money was front and center *all the time*. Dollar signs loomed in every conversation. I could barely think about anything else.

It didn't help that I was bleeding financially. As the agreements we'd made at the negotiating table started to play out in real time, the child support, alimony payments, and maintenance on the family house started to add up. My divorce was costing me close to $1,000 a week—and that didn't even touch my own living expenses.

For a long time, all I could do was put on my blinders and focus on rebuilding financially. However, it didn't work as well as I'd hoped. A year or so in, I finally had to admit that my money woes weren't going to be over anytime soon. More money wasn't really the answer, anyway; I'd been there, done that, and divorced it. I wanted prosperity, sure—but I wanted it on my own terms, across my whole life, not just in my bank account. I wanted to *feel* like I had prosperity, not just *look* like I did.

Okay, great. Cue the congratulatory music, cut to stage left. I'd figured out what I wanted; the light bulb had switched on. But I still had no idea how to get there from where I was.

Looking for a first step, I started asking myself why prosperity and security are so tangled up with money, especially when it comes to divorce. The answer I came up with is that money, to most people, *is* security. And in divorce, not only does the relationship implode, the financial structures you built as a couple also crumble. Everything gets torn apart and rearranged.

Money can function as a cushion between all of the sadness, grief, and loss that comes with divorce and the paralyzing terror of being unable to fulfill basic needs for yourself and your family. Let's face it: you can only process so much crap at once. It's a lot easier to navigate your emotions and grieve the end of your relationship when you're not worried about how to pay your mortgage and put food on the table.

When money is front and center, and the future is uncertain, that nasty, grasping fear about the loss of basic security and identity comes rushing to the surface, and it puts its grimy hands on *everything*.

In any divorce—even an amicable one—money is the chief topic of discussion. A big chunk of the divorce process is figuring out how to divide the assets, remortgage the house, pay for the kids' expenses, distribute the debt, etc. Unless you're a millionaire (and maybe even then), splitting up the finances is going to cause one or both parties real strain, and rattle the foundation of security—shaky as it might already have been— that the marriage and joint assets once provided.

And so, when we talk about money in the context of divorce,

we're not just talking about cash, properties, and investments. We're talking about people's *deepest fears and feelings* about security, identity, and self-worth. Talking about money becomes like prodding an open wound, and fear becomes like an infection.

Most people, in the chaos of divorce, aren't aware enough to see that they're actually dealing with *emotions*, not assets. They wonder why their ex has suddenly turned into a complete a-hole and keeps blowing his lid over nothing, or why a partner who was never stingy with money suddenly hoards every red cent—but they can't see all the stuff happening below the surface. They may not even recognize what's happening inside themselves. They just know that every time the lawyers say the words "retirement accounts," the temperature in the room drops ten degrees, and they want to bite someone's head off.

In divorce, women are statistically more likely than men to make emotional decisions rather than rational ones. It's in our nature. Either we want the divorce to be over as quickly as possible—not just for our own sake, but for everyone's—or we want everything that made us feel secure to stay exactly as it was before the relationship ended, and so fight like a mama badger to hold on to what we feel is rightly ours, even if we'd be best served by letting it go. Whichever side we fall on, the more uncertain and fearful we feel, the more we want to "just get it over with," and the more we are bothered by anything that prolongs the process.

Anisa was married to an alcoholic for more than ten years. Her ability to hold it all together for her kids and create a safe space for them no longer existed. She could no longer shield her kids from the mornings of Daddy vomiting as they got ready for school, or evenings of rage-filled outbursts when he finally came home. He had been out of work for more than two years, and was unwilling to look for work or get help for his addiction. It was too much to bear, and so she made the difficult decision to file for divorce.

As the sole provider in the home, she had a stable job with benefits, money in her bank account, and a retirement plan. She knew her life would be better without all the drama and pain her family was experiencing, and she felt confident that she would be able to provide for her kids even once he was out of the house. After all, he wasn't contributing any income.

As they moved through the mediation process, Anisa decided that she didn't want to leave her children's father destitute. She wanted to be fair; after all, "fair and equitable" was the basis on which the courts decided the separation of assets, right? More, she didn't want to pay a lawyer to fight on her behalf if things got ugly. This set her up to get taken advantage of in a big way.

Because she wanted to keep the house, she had to get a home equity loan to pay him the $38,000 which was his share of the equity. Okay, that seemed fair. Then, since he had only just secured a part-time job, he insisted that she take on 100 percent of the credit card debt—more than $8,000, most of it accrued in the two years he'd been out of work. She agreed.

As the primary caretaker, the kids would be with her most of the time. He agreed to pay $90 a week in child support per the State Support Guidelines, but argued that he would not pay toward the kids' health insurance costs because she earned more than he did. She agreed.

In the third session, he asked for his share of her retirement savings. If she didn't give it to him, he would hire a lawyer and take her to court—so she conceded 25 percent of her retirement assets.

Every time Anisa stepped into that mediation room, she was overwhelmed by the feeling of just wanting it to be over. She convinced herself that she could, and would, recoup what she was losing; it was more important to close the proceedings as quickly as possible, so he couldn't add anything else to his list of wants or fly off the handle when something he asked for was denied. She kept reminding herself that the ultimate goal was to get divorced, not come out richer than her ex.

Walking into the courtroom, she wasn't thinking about her future security. She only knew that, once that gavel dropped, she would finally be free of the man who was making her life miserable. It was a race to the finish.

Women like Anisa who are leaving abusive relationships, are even more likely than most to sacrifice their future financial well-being in order to get away from their ex. Worn down by aggression or manipulation, they just want their freedom, and will sacrifice whatever they need to in order to get it. Others simply feel guilty or selfish about focusing on the money aspect of divorce, and don't want to "play the bitch card" by taking a stand for what is rightfully theirs. These tendencies set women up to be victimized by their circumstances later on, when they realize that they gave away too much, or didn't think about life beyond D-Day.

Here's the hard truth: as long as shared assets are a central part of marriage, money is always going to be the central focus of divorce. You can't change the facts—and if you ignore them, you'll only end up hurting yourself.

When Anisa reached out to me, she was one year post-divorce and drowning financially. She hadn't taken the time to figure out how much her concessions would actually cost her before agreeing to them—and her ex had pulled the plug on child support after he lost his job.

Her e-mail to me went something like this:

Hi, Michelle. My mom has been encouraging me to reach out to you for some time now. I'm recently divorced and receiving no child support. I'm paying everything on time, but by the skin of my teeth. I really need some advice about how I can dig myself out of this ever-growing hole!

Anisa's "hole" was close to $1,200 a month, every month. If she didn't change something, she was going to go bankrupt. We immediately sat down to look at the realities of the situation and make a new plan. The truth was, she couldn't keep going as though nothing had changed. She needed to redesign her life around the realities of her divorce.

Today, while things have not been completely linear, she has a sense of control and confidence. We consolidated her various credit card debts into a fixed-rate personal loan, lowering her monthly expenses by $616. We also created a workable budget that gives her a structural view of her plan and incorporated a fun tool to track her spending, ensuring she is successful at staying within her planned boundaries. To improve her bottom line, she also took on a side hustle doing direct sales in addition to her teaching job; this has earned her an extra $12,000 over the past twenty-two months, kept her kids in their respective sports, and added to her emergency fund and her sense of stability.

If you are currently in the middle of a divorce, my advice to you is to stop, take a breath, and get a handle on the facts of the situation. The more frenzied your emotions, the more this divorce will cost you—mentally, physically, and financially— and the further from your vision of prosperity you'll be when the smoke clears. If your divorce is already behind you, and you're dealing with the aftermath, your journey to prosperity will start the moment you get real with yourself over where you are and how you got there. Only then can you make a plan to redesign your life and create the prosperity and security you want.

Why Getting a Handle on Your Money is Vital to Prosperity After Divorce

Divorce forces us to ask the hardest question of our lives:

"What I am worth?"

This question is both practical and spiritual, and the answer to one side can influence the other.

Of course, money doesn't determine your worth as a person (even if it feels that way sometimes). But the way you relate to your money and your net worth can teach you a lot about how you value yourself, and how you can create real prosperity after divorce.

As women, we're often taught that it's not polite or appropriate to talk about money. Sometimes, this results in us avoiding tough discussions or joint decision-making; other times, it results in us handing over the financial reins entirely. When this happens, we might suddenly discover that we're lacking five, ten, even twenty years of in-depth knowledge about our own finances!

When you avoid money—when you don't talk about it, or let other people control it for you—you're literally putting your "worth" in someone else's hands. When the time comes to make decisions about what you want and need in a divorce settlement, you may find yourself with absolutely no idea what's happening. You may also seriously mis-estimate the amount of money that is rightfully yours under the law.

Getting this part wrong can cost you tens of thousands of dollars; in high-net-worth divorces, it can cost millions. It can also deal a harsh blow to your self-esteem and self-reliance.

I don't say this to scare you; I say it because getting an accurate financial picture is vital and necessary to prosperity after divorce. You need to muster the courage to take an objective, clear look at your finances, so you can make sound decisions about what you need and are entitled to. What will your living costs be? Will there be direct or indirect changes to health insurance, mortgages, retirement funding, and other expenses? What is your plan if the support your ex agrees to doesn't come through?

If your divorce is already finalized, you need to take a look at the reality of your situation. What income and/or support were you expecting? What are you actually receiving? What habits need to be changed? What do you need to do in order to feel secure?

I'll teach you more about assessing your living costs and planning around your new income in Chapters Four and Five, but I want you to start thinking about this now. Why? Because the sooner you start getting real about your money, the sooner you can start redesigning your life and taking steps toward the version of prosperity you want.

Don't put this on the back burner. This is your *life* we're talking about!

Your life is going to be different after a divorce whether you like it or not. So do yourself a favor, and start getting specific about those differences right now. Today. It doesn't matter if you're in the middle of divorcing, or if your divorce is a decade behind you: if you're not living your version of prosperity, and you want to make a change, you need to start by truly seeing where you are. Then, you can make a plan based on reality, not on what you think is going on or what you wish your life looked like.

I wish someone had given me this advice when I was in the middle of my own divorce. Like Anisa, I just wanted it over with. And, quite honestly, even if I'd wanted help in this area, I wouldn't have known who to turn to. My lawyer certainly didn't offer anything in this regard. I just kept on living the same old way—only now I was in a totally different life. Sometimes, I want to reach back through time, shake myself, and shriek, "Stop! What are you *doing*?"

Well, to be honest, what I was doing was trying to use money to create security.

WHAT "SECURITY" REALLY MEANS

Regardless of how carefully you plan, or how affluent you are, your security is going to be challenged in your divorce.

Security comes in many forms: physical, emotional, mental, spiritual, and financial. What's more, your personal experience of prosperity is directly tied to your definition of security.

Developing a deep understanding of your personal definition of prosperity should be at the top of your divorce work. When you feel prosperous, you also feel secure—but security looks different for everyone.

So, ask yourself: Is my security tied to money and possessions? Is it tied to love and relationships? Is it tied to time, stability, or freedom? Understanding this will give you a platform from which you can make sound decisions about your new life. This is important because, no matter how you define security, it will almost certainly be challenged by your divorce.

Katie had moved out of the marital home and into a nice three-bedroom apartment. She and her soon-to-be-ex had agreed to a 50/50 split schedule with the kids, and she wasn't receiving support while mediation was taking place, but she felt she would be fine. Her rent was only half of what her mortgage had been, and her ex had agreed to cover the overhead at the house as long as she paid half the taxes.

I watched the first six months unfold with a sort of awe. On the nights Katie didn't have the kids, she was out with friends, indulging in fancy dinners and shopping sprees. She purchased a new convertible, saying, "I don't have the overhead of the house now, and I want to feel my independence on every sunny day I can!" On the weekends, she and the kids had "Sunday Fun-Days," going to Red Sox games, concerts, fairs, water parks, and anyplace else that caught their interest. She also replaced the annual family camping trip with an all-inclusive Caribbean resort vacation.

While she felt secure at first about her decisions to take life up a notch—"After so many years," she told me, "I'm finally happy, and the kids seem to love our adventures. Isn't that the most important thing right now?"—it wasn't long before her new highs started to take her to new lows. Rather than letting her already-depleted savings dip to an emergency level, she started to use her credit cards. Soon, her biweekly paychecks were no longer enough to meet her basic obligations. She'd run her credit card up to its $15,000 limit and had just applied for another card.

"How did this happen?" she asked me.

The issue wasn't just that Katie was spending money like a drunken sailor on Saturday night. It was that she was coming from a space of emotional decision-making. She hadn't sat down pre-divorce—or even post-divorce—to figure out how much money she actually had, and what she could truly afford to spend on little luxuries like clothes, meals out, and outings with the kids (never mind big luxuries, like the vacation). If she had taken the time to do that, and committed to living within her means and planning for the luxuries she wanted (instead of trying to acquire them all at once), she wouldn't have ended up broke with a $15,000 credit card bill hanging over her head.

By trying to buy security, Katie actually made herself and her situation more insecure. This is the paradox of emotional decision-making, and the price of failing to understand what drives our personal sense of security. Katie's definition of security is tied into financial abundance, but also freedom and adventure. Her mistake wasn't in trying to create those things for herself, but rather trying to create them in a way that gave her *less* freedom and financial stability, not more.

I offered to take a look at her finances and help her see what her post-divorce financial life actually needed to look like. "We need to completely redesign your finances," I told her. "Are you ready for this?"

"I haven't wanted to look at the money until now," she confessed. "I was afraid that if I knew what I was in for, I might not have had the courage to leave my marriage."

This fear of scarcity is at the root at a lot of "avoidance behavior" in divorce. I had indulged in it myself, so I knew exactly where Katie was coming from, and was able to create a safe space of non-judgment for her as she worked through her money issues.

My own security is tied to time and freedom—but I spent the first couple of years after my divorce trying to purchase a feeling of stability. I was working sixty hours a week to get back on track, and since I was now responsible for my kids' schedules as well as my own (that had been my ex's job before the split), I had less free time than ever. After a year or more of this craziness, I finally realized that my kids didn't want a mom who was little more than a walking cash machine or a chauffeur. They wanted a mom who was *present*, and who prioritized them beyond rides to activities and sports. They were angry, confused, and too damn busy, and so was I. More, I wasn't giving them what they needed by spending more money on them—and I wasn't feeling any more "secure," either.

I craved being a better mom to them. I craved that time on the sidelines at their games, the moments when their eyes met mine over the heads of the crowd. I wanted to be the mom who rode the bus with them on field trips so I could share in the adventure. But my quest for financial stability was getting in the way of all of that. I was creating *my* prosperity after divorce, but what about theirs?

One morning, as I sat quietly in prayer, this thought came to mind: "Maybe prosperity is me making a decision that money isn't the only component of prosperity. Maybe prosperity is me putting my kids first, and taking the time I've been craving to just be with them."

All of a sudden, I understood: divorce was about money, but prosperity didn't have to be. Healing and empowerment wouldn't come to me or my kids through more money, more work time, or more stuff. Instead, I had to *create* prosperity every day by feeling and exploring every part of my personal definition of security, not just the financial.

Like magic, once I started prioritizing the other elements that defined security for me—time and freedom—the weight of the financial stuff seemed to lift.

The Bottom Line

Defining what security and prosperity look like *for you* is the most important work you can do during and after a divorce.

Don't avoid this work. Don't procrastinate because you're too busy, or avoid the subject because it makes you uncomfortable. If you want to create prosperity after divorce, you need to know exactly what you're shooting for, so you don't waste time wandering in circles, replaying old patterns and making the same old mistakes.

Then, you need to figure out where you stand *right now*, at this moment, even if you don't like it, or you wish it was different. Only then can you figure out a plan to get from Point A (where you are now) to Point P (your version of prosperity after divorce).

Right now, you might not feel prosperous at all. You might feel sad, anxious, guilty, stressed, and downright scared. That's okay. It's totally normal and healthy to feel those things—one at a time, or all at once! (That said, if you're having a lot of trouble processing your feelings, or if you're experiencing symptoms of depression, anxiety, or other mental health issues, it's a good idea to seek professional help.) Regardless of how hard things are in this moment, you're not going to feel like this forever. So stop, take a breath, grab your journal, and ask yourself:

"What does my prosperity look like?"

You may get a vision right away, like watching a movie scene. Or, you may just get a general "feeling." Either way, write down what comes to you. Flesh it out as much as possible. Imagine yourself living your ideal day. What are you doing? Who are you with?

The rest of this book is full of tools to help you define, refine, and implement your vision of prosperity. (Like I mentioned in Chapter One, this is all done through the lens of finance, since that's my shtick, but since money touches all areas of life, we'll have the opportunity to explore prosperity in many incarnations.) The "how" of your prosperity will come later; for now, just focus on defining what you want. Write it down. Make a vision board. Pick a mantra. Do what you've gotta do to connect with what you want in your new life.

Your vision for prosperity after divorce will be your starting place for all of the work we'll do together in the rest of this book.

In the next chapter, we'll explore the basic steps you'll need to take to get started on the path to a redesigned life and prosperity after divorce ... but first, the story of how I almost lost it all, and instead found an amazing new life.

Chapter Three

FINDING THE WAY FORWARD

---◆◈◆---

B ob, my genius therapist, reminded me regularly that, in every season, something must die in order for something new to be born.

I thought about that a lot. It certainly felt some days like my old life was in its death throes. So much was the same— my job, my car, my clothes—and yet, my life was completely different than it had been before.

I had no idea that my decision to divorce would cause so much change. I know it sounds naïve, but it's true: I pictured our lives going on pretty much as they had before, just without my ex-husband. I pictured my kids having not one, but two safe and loving homes. I pictured my ex and I co-parenting, raising the kids according to the same values and principles we'd adhered to together. I envisioned us at our son's games and our daughter's school functions, sitting in different bleachers but both cheering them on.

Yeah, not so much.

Our two-days-on, two-days-off schedule was taxing for all of us. I was working sixty hours a week to pay for our divorce and my slew of new living expenses, and my ex was reentering the workforce after a seven-year sabbatical at home raising the kids. Our old routines were nonexistent.

My amazing mom stepped in with huge amounts of grandma love: she greeted the kids with hugs and smiles when they got off the bus (at either house), carted them to and from sports practices, dentist visits, and doctor's appointments. She fed them dinner when I had to work late, and stayed with them when I had to travel. She was my rock, and I think my ex would say the same.

But despite all of our efforts, that first year of transition was not easy. My son, always outspoken, wanted a commitment that I would change my mind and bring our family back together. My daughter took the brunt of his pain, and tried her best to soften his tears. At fifteen, she was well beyond her years already: she was the one who kept it all inside. She managed to keep up as a straight-A student, co-captain of the varsity cheerleading squad, and family peacemaker.

I knew my daughter could see my fears ratcheting higher and higher as I worked crazy hours to meet my personal and business obligations. I know she could see her father slipping deeper into depression, and numbing with booze every night. I wanted to protect her from this—from what *I* had caused, my guilt told me—but I couldn't. In our new life situation, it was what it was.

And yet, paradoxically, at the same time as we were struggling to adjust to our new family paradigm, I felt like I was becoming more "me" than I had ever been. I no longer had to pull a personality shift when I pulled into the driveway at the end of the day. I could give my kids the real me, not the me who made my ex comfortable. I tried my best to find joy in the journey, and—with my mom's help—even managed to find a few minutes here and there to have a personal life.

Toward the end of that first year, I decided I was ready to start dating. My ex had met someone new, and while I wasn't ready to get serious with anyone yet, I did feel like it was time to dive back in. Not long after that, I met Jody, the man who is now my partner. Long story short, I felt like I had connected with my true soulmate. Within six months, we decided that we were ready to be together on a more permanent basis. We found a God-struck home on ten acres with enough bedrooms for our entire blended family. My kids could stay in their school as long as I drove them every day.

THE UNIVERSE STARTS KNOCKING

My old life was dying away. My new life was being born. I had never felt so hopeful.

But while bliss was blossoming on our side, things were spiraling downward at my old house. My ex's girlfriend had moved in with her kids, and the situation was toxic. She was the opposite of both me and my ex in that she liked conflict, and wanted to fight things out, even if it meant doing so in front of the kids. My ex started to drink more, use drugs more, escape more—and the kids were left to witness the fallout.

As you can imagine, the stress level was running high— especially for my daughter, the natural caretaker in the family. At the beginning of her junior year, she started getting debilitating migraines that kept her confined to her dark bedroom for two to three days at a time. From September to January, she missed fifty-two days of school. My focus (in between working a shitload of hours to keep my business running) was to try to get to the root of the problem. We tested alternative therapy options as well as half a dozen medications, but nothing seemed to help. More, she no longer wanted to be moved from home to home while she was sick. She liked the quiet of our new country house, and didn't want to go back to the craziness at her dad's. (Of course, this caused a lot of friction between me and my ex.)

The mama in me felt so sad that I had to leave her each morning to go to work. She encouraged me to go, saying, "There's nothing you can do for me, Mom, except let me rest. It's okay." But I knew that, deep down, she wanted me by her side, even if she wouldn't say it. I felt like I was letting her down—and that was a gut blow.

Eight months into this health nightmare, I received a frightening call at 9:30 p.m. on a Tuesday. Jody had just called to say that he was coming home and was fifteen minutes away. As I fired up the grill for our dinner, I heard the fire siren go off, but didn't think much of it. Then, two minutes later, I received another call from an out-of-state number.

They say we have a "sixth sense" about our loved ones, and that we know, somehow, when they are in danger. That's exactly the feeling that came over me as I looked at the unknown number on my phone. I didn't pick up; instead, I called my boyfriend's line. He didn't answer.

When the odd number called back a moment later, I answered.

"Hello, is this Michelle?"

"Yes, why?" I demanded. "What's going on?"

She explained that Jody had been involved in an accident and had given her my number to call since I was expecting him. Good Samaritan that he is, he had stopped to help someone else who had been in an accident, and had been hit and thrown by another car.

Her voice was calm—but then, I heard Jody screaming in the background. I lost it, rattling off a hundred questions to which this poor woman had no answers. Finally, I hung up in frustration, and called my cousin who worked in the local emergency room, to see if he had any news.

"It just came in over the scanner. Not sure if there are any fatalities, but it sounds serious," he said. "The best thing I can tell you is to stand on your deck and listen for the LifeStar helicopter. I'll call you back in a few minutes when I know more so I can tell you where to go."

Yeah, right. Not going to happen.

I packed my daughter into the car and sped toward the accident scene. The road was closed a mile before the actual scene, and the cops wouldn't let us through. They suggested I head to the hospital and meet the ambulance there.

When I got to the ER, my mom was already there, murmuring to Jody and holding his hand. He was in major pain (getting hit by a car going forty miles per hour will do that) but very much alive. I sobbed in relief.

I spent the next five days trying to figure out a way to keep Jody in our home while he waited for the surgery he needed to rebuild his knees and ligaments. I spent days unable to think about business, answer client e-mails, or take phone calls. I could literally feel the Universe whispering in my ear, "You have to step up, Michelle." I thought it meant that I had to do more, do everything. But it wasn't possible! My nose was already to the grindstone. I had nothing left—but I was too scared to contemplate what this might mean, so I just kept going, and going, and going.

The next six months were pure hell. I went back to working sixty hours a week just one week after Jody's accident. My daughter was at home learning from tutors, and with the pressure of showing up for school off the table, she was doing better—but she still got at least one major migraine per week. We had to sort out who was going to run Jody's business while he was recovering. And I was still spinning a hundred plates, trying to make it all work.

What got us through was the incredible support we received from family and friends. With every visit there were offers to help. We had so many visitors at the hospital in those first three days that the greeter, a seventy-five-year-old volunteer, thought they had admitted a small-town celebrity—and, in a way, they had. My man had always put out a hand to anyone who needed it, and was the guy who took the time to call to check up on someone if he knew they were having a rough day. It was beautiful for him, and for our family to have the same. Also amazing were the friends who offered to build a handicap ramp to our front door, drop off meals, mow our lawn, and sit with Jody so I could go back to work.

Yes, work. That looming specter. It was the one thing that hadn't changed in the whirlwind of my life post-divorce.

Work couldn't remain a second priority for me for long. My role in my company was outside commercial sales; I was the hunter and gatherer of new business, making new connections and delivering quotes to keep our new and current clients happy and up to speed. I was blessed to have a service manager who was the Batman to my Robin, the yin to my yang— but she could only shoulder so much of my workload before the business started to suffer.

My days ran into nights as I was now not only managing my and my kids' schedules, but also my guy's physical therapy appointments. I worked from 6:30 a.m. until 5:00 p.m. on Saturdays, and the same on Sundays. Actually, there were no more days and nights; I filled all but four hours a day with work and other responsibilities.

I was breaking. I was exhausted. I felt like I was being punished and, for the first time, I was starting to resent my business like it was an ex-lover. Because of my workload, I was unable to give my family what they needed, and instead had to lean heavily on others to pull off the things I should have been doing myself. Once again, my mother stepped in to do what she could while I shouldered these new challenges, but I could see her exhaustion as well.

I started getting chest pains bad enough to wake me in the middle of the night from a sound sleep. When I found a few moments to pray or meditate, I kept getting a clear message that something had to change. My family needed more from me, and I needed more from life. I had to step up—and not in the way I had been doing. But how?

Then, an epiphany. I couldn't change my daughter's situation. I couldn't make my partner heal faster. I couldn't change the circumstances of my divorce settlement. But ... could I possibly change my career?

My whole being rebelled at the thought. My work was my entire security; it was the one constant amidst all the change of the past few years. It provided everything for us, all our basic needs: food, shelter, health insurance. More, it provided my ability to keep my financial commitments to my former spouse, and the extra funds to sneak in a few days of vacation here and there so I could muster the mental and physical stamina to keep going. I had just celebrated twenty-three years in my industry, and I had never once questioned my commitment to it. I thought I loved what I did—but did I? What, exactly, did I love about it?

THE SHIFT BEGINS

Interestingly, not long after I started asking these tough questions, I met Deb, a life coach, at a networking group one morning. She was sweet, energetic, a "refugee" from Corporate America who had reinvented herself. I stepped away from our conversation thinking that maybe I had just met my long-lost sister, and did my mom have something to tell me? I resolved to call her—and then promptly got busy, and forgot.

A few weeks later, I was having lunch with a friend, venting about my stress level and my desire to change *something*. My friend smiled, and handed me a business card.

"You owe it to yourself to figure this out!" she told me. "We're not leaving until you call this woman."

The card, of course, was Deb's.

I had never considered a coach. I had also never hired a personal trainer. The reality was, I had never considered investing in myself for anything. Sure, my business partner and I sent ourselves and our staff to professional development weekends and team-building seminars, and I'd spent thousands on personal development books, CDs, and online programs, but this was different.

Seriously? I said to myself. *A life coach? Who do you think you are, some celebrity?*

But those chest pains were scaring me, and I was hanging by a thread. Something had to give.

My first meeting with Deb was a "discovery session" to see if working together made sense. We exchanged niceties and then dove right in. I couldn't believe how easily I opened up.

I asked her if she had any psychic skills. "Why spend weeks talking about this stuff when we can cut to the chase, right?" I joked.

Deb laughed, and said that, while she was not, in fact, a clairvoyant, she was great at working with people so they could gain clarity and meet their goals.

"So," she countered. "What *are* your goals?"

The answer came easily. "Decompression. I want to take off my Superwoman cape and not worry that my world will fall down around me."

She didn't even blink at my intensity. That calm, settled energy was so inviting to me. I wanted what she had.

We met at the park for our sessions—"So you can take care of yourself in more than one way while we work," she said. Over the next several weeks, I began to walk softer and lighter. I looked at my business and realized where I was taking too much on myself and ignoring the places where my team could grow. Just asking simple questions like "Why?" and "Why not?" got me thinking in a whole new way. I made a plan to change my company structure to better support both me and our clients.

After six weeks, Deb asked me to step out of the practical and start to dream a little more. "Tell me, Michelle, what does your ideal work day look like? How about your ideal weekday evening? Your ideal weekend?"

"Does 'ideal' exist for business owners?" I quipped. But inside, I knew this was big. This was me defining my prosperity.

The Big Ideals

I had a four-day vacation planned with my kids before our next session, so I decided to take her assignment with me.

On day one, I did … nothing. On day, two, nothing. Annoyed, I went over my reality in my head, but my notebook remained blank.

At the beach that day, I realized that in order to answer Deb's assignment of "ideals," I had to stop thinking and start dreaming. *Does she give this assignment to others?* I wondered. *Do they just write, or do they struggle too?* It didn't matter; I wanted to get it done. So on day four, I awoke committed to dreaming.

Watching the morning sunrise over the ocean with my first cup of coffee in hand, I sat in a space of complete gratitude. I had just spent three amazing days with Jody and our kids, laughing, playing in the ocean, and indulging in numerous games of UNO and fireside s'mores in the evening. I hadn't raised my voice in four days. I hadn't rushed them out the door barking my agenda. My son and I sat together and cuddled for what seemed like the first time in months.

This is my first ideal, I thought. *More cuddling. More love. More bliss. What would that look like at home?*

The first thought that came to mind is that I would have to change our chaotic morning routine. I would have to stop projecting my agenda, which always seemed to be coming out of my mouth between 7:30 and 7:45 a.m. as I was rushing my son to gather his things so I could have him at school by 8:01, and get to my office—a thirty-minute ride away—by 8:31. Our mornings were beyond stressful. I had a boy who had never had to be dragged out of bed, and who did his homework without ever being told—but our mornings were filled with

"Hurry up! We are going to end up behind the bus if you're not in the car in thirty seconds!" By the time we burst out the door, I had already been awake for two hours, making lunches, folding laundry, unloading dishes, and figuring out dinner. On top of all that, I'd already trekked my daughter to school at 6:45 a.m. and booked it home again. When I got home from the first school run, my son had already gathered his things and fed himself, but I still pushed him to move faster because I was always rushing.

What would a calmer morning look like? A morning of loving discussion and hugs goodbye? Our truth was so far from my ideal that it broke my heart. Tears ran down my face as I realized that I had created this "normal" for us.

Then, I heard a soft voice whisper, "What if you got to the office at nine o'clock instead?"

Well, I was dreaming, after all, so I might as well write it down. *Ideal #1: Start work later.*

Next, I realized that I was sad that I kept missing my son's games. He was a three-sport athlete, and I was *that* mom who only showed up for the first and last games of the season. If you asked me what position he played, I would answer, "offense," because I didn't know.

Again, that encouraging voice spoke: "Dream, Michelle. What is your ideal?"

I wrote. *Ideal #2: Be at my kids' games.*

I continued with my list, and when I was finished I had finished Deb's homework assignment. I had a complete picture of what my ideal life would look like. I knew that, if I wanted to create even a fraction of what I wanted, a lot would have to change. But I could do this. I would just have to start small. I tucked away my journal and went upstairs, where the kids had been throwing pillows at one another for the last thirty minutes. This was my last day to enjoy them before we went back to "normal," and I intended to enjoy this sacred, noisy, chaotic family time.

My session with Deb was just a few days after I returned from vacation. I was excited to be able to hand her my "list"and know I had finished.

"How did it go?" she asked.

"It took me eleven days to write a single thing down," I admitted.

"Interesting," she replied.

Yes, interesting it was.

I started booking my first clients at 9:30 instead of 8:30 each morning. No one seemed to care, or even notice. Emboldened, I started confining my client interactions to two days a week between 9 a.m. and 2 p.m.—but that didn't go so well. There was simply too much to do, and we didn't have the staff for me to delegate to. If I wanted to create my ideal, I would have to solve this problem.

The other internal struggle I was facing was around how implementing these changes might look in my business partnership. After seventeen years, our roles were clearly defined, and I wasn't sure the change I wanted would work for everyone involved. *Much like in a marriage*, I reflected. Honestly, I was scared that any major changes to our "normal" would land me in another divorce. And, given what I'd been through in the last two years, why in God's name would I want to do that?

Working through this bit by bit, I realized that what I wanted wasn't a change to the amazing business and culture my partner and I had built over seventeen years. I wanted a change in the fabric of my life. I wanted simplicity. I wanted more space. I wanted my version of prosperity after divorce.

Most of all, I wanted a different kind of security. I had been so focused on rebuilding financially that I had chosen my business over my family. And no amount of money was worth that.

I couldn't wait until I finally mastered the work-life balance thing. That would be like trying to master healthy eating when you're already having a heart attack. By the time I managed it, it would be too late, and my kids would be grown and off to college. I needed a drastic shift and a massive reprioritization. I needed to stop *trying* to fix things, and actually *fix* them.

And that could only happen one way. I needed to step away from my business.

I booked a few days off from work to spend with the kids, just to test the waters. Of course, it was amazing. The kids were practically jumping up and down when they saw me on the sidelines. The other parents had no idea who I was, but that didn't matter. I was there.

And that was what gave me the validation I needed. I wanted this—this time, this freedom. That was what felt like prosperity for me.

Over the next few months, I worked with Deb on my exit plan. Basically, I had to prepare my staff and my business partner to operate without me. I was committed to the continued success of the business, and I loved my staff; I had no desire to see anyone stumble because of my decisions.

And so, my plan was hatched: I wrote the details out on my thick yellow pad. My business partner's daughters who had worked tirelessly for more than seventeen years with us in the business, could buy me out, and split my shares 50/50. I would then stay on for one year to supervise the transition and make sure everyone felt solid with the new structure.

The day I approached my business partner with this new plan, ideals list in hand, was one of the hardest of my life— but everything in my being told me it was the right thing to do. My partner was shocked at first, but totally supportive. We ended up coming to an arrangement that benefited us both. She made the transition even easier by agreeing to buy me out and figuring things out with her daughters later on. On New Year's Eve—six months earlier than expected—I said goodbye to the business that was as much my baby as my own children.

My last day at the office was bittersweet—not happy, not sad. It seemed as though everyone else went about the day like it was any other day—but it certainly wasn't an ordinary day for me. I spent those final hours going back through the processes and procedure manuals I had worked up to make sure I hadn't missed even the smallest instruction that might be needed by the new support staffer, and making sure that the next six months of client renewals were mapped out. As I sat alone in my office, my emotions welled up as I realized that I would no longer greet the girls as I walked through the doors in the morning, or swap stories about our kids at the lunch table. I would no longer have my Diet Pepsi dropped on my desk each morning by a co-worker who shared my habit. I would no longer need my cape, because I was passing it on.

In just twenty-four hours, I would open my calendar to show a new year, and there would be no entries.

I would wake up with no agenda. No schedule. I could eat breakfast—something I rarely had time for. I could take a yoga class or join a gym. I could watch the snow fall and not care that it was going to mess up my morning schedule. I could do whatever I wanted! And, because I'd been bought out of my shares of the business, I didn't have to worry about how I was going to take care of my family. My years of hard work had paid off, and there was nothing but possibility in front of me.

It was awesome. And scary as hell.

PERSONAL TRAINING

While all of this was going on, I was (unbeknownst to me) training myself to step into a new life, a new business, and a new version of myself.

I had been leading the Financial Peace University classes at my church for about six months before all of this change unfolded. I loved helping others get free from debt and re-establish their financial footing. I was even asked to attend a class in Nashville offered by financial guru Dave Ramsey for his coordinators. Despite everything else I had going on, I felt compelled to say yes. After all, I had always had a love for teaching others.

When I got to Nashville, I was in for a big surprise. I had actually been signed up for "Counselor training," not "Coordinator training." I was swept up into an intense, boot camp-style certification program focused on one-on-one financial coaching rather than class and workshop facilitation. I rolled my eyes at first, thinking I was wasting my time, but I was already there, so I might as well stay, right?

The next four days were filled with intensity. Case studies, peer work, homework, group assessments … and amazing growth on my part. I even got to meet Dave Ramsey and spend time with him and his team. I loved every minute of it. I also knew that God had his hand in moving me in this direction. In the first sessions, I chuckled to myself, thinking, *If I had known what I was in for here, I would never have signed up!*

"I know that," the quiet voice replied. "So I got you here anyway."

I came back from that four-day event with a certificate declaring that I was now a Dave Ramsey Trained Independent Financial Counselor. I felt a strong sense of purpose, as though

I had been chosen to work in this area. I was being shown a path. I had no idea what it would look like, but I would take Dave and his team up on their challenge to see one client in the next ten days.

I offered to work with one of the couples in my class who were struggling with implementation. She had been diagnosed with cancer and was no longer working while she sought treatment. That meant that their family had unexpectedly lost almost $1,800 a month in income and were truly upside down at the end of each month. I provided perspective, options, and hard decisions to consider so they wouldn't lose everything they had worked so hard for, including their home. The work was emotional but purposeful; I felt grateful to be able to be part of the solution for this struggling couple.

After I sold my share in my business, the idea of coaching people who were in financial difficulty came up again. And when the time came to start creating a new avenue of work for myself, I knew just what I wanted to do.

THE BIG SHIFT

When you think about your "ideals," your first priorities should be healing and empowerment. These are the things that will connect you to your prosperity. As my story proves, if you make choices only around finances, you will never feel prosperous.

That said, when you're ready to connect to your personal version of prosperity after divorce, you're going to have to look at the money. Like we talked about in Chapter Two, divorce is all about money. More, divorce is all about what money—and security—mean to you.

It took me awhile to get comfortable in the new skin I was

wearing. It took longer to turn off the guilt tapes that kept replaying in my mind. *Why hadn't I done this sooner? What was I thinking? How much time did my stubbornness cost me?*

Looking backward isn't productive, because it doesn't help you change anything. You need to be willing to lift the veil and look with total clarity at where you are today and where you want to be in your ideal life.

I needed support to do this, and space to process all of my tangled fears and emotions. What Deb did for me, I now do for other women, through the lens of dollars and cents. We all have different stories about divorce, and different life situations, but our need to heal and move forward is the same. The stories shared in my Prosperity After Divorce Facebook group prove this to me again and again.

As we take the reins of our own development, we need to be willing to dig deep into the major areas of our life—the areas that will forever be changed not just by our divorce, but by the choices we make about our prosperity after divorce. Whether we like it or not, life as we know is never going to be the same. It doesn't mean worse. It just means different.

The thing is, I was really, really lucky. My choice to change my life didn't ruin us financially. Much of this was simply good planning; I've always been a saver, despite my expensive tastes, and selling my share of the business gave me a pretty amazing nest egg. I realize that you may not be in a similar situation—and if you're panicking about your finances, it can make the decision to live in your prosperity even harder. I understand this, and I see it all the time with my clients. But current financial struggle is no excuse for putting your quest for prosperity on hold. In fact, it makes it all the more imperative.

When I started my practice as a Financial Coach, I noticed that women would come to me with their financial struggles in all stages of divorce and post-divorce. Some were struggling to make ends meet. Others had "enough," but wanted to be empowered to make the right choices for themselves and their families so they could become, and stay, prosperous according to their own ideals. Although our time together included creating workable budgets around bills and due dates, I was also able to create a wider view for these women around their current lifestyle and what it would take to sustain it or grow in the direction of their new dream.

During our sessions, not only were we working on their "money stuff," we were redesigning their lifestyles! While we crunched numbers, we were having discussions about their daily challenges around work, kids, family support (or lack thereof), and friends who had split off from their lives. There were many conversations about the desire to stop grieving, wake up, and start living. As they gained their footing, these resilient women were empowered because they had a concrete plan they could tweak, twist, and change as their lives continued to evolve. More importantly, they had a sense of knowing exactly where they were, where they wanted to go, and what they needed to do to get there. For the first time in months, years, or decades, they were in charge of their money, their security, and their lives.

Take my client Teresa, who came to me two years post-divorce. When we met, she was so far in denial about her current situation that she was literally living in an alternate reality. She just kept shopping and shopping. She would stay up every night watching QVC, then swiping "buy now" from the app on her phone. Rather than going out to the store, she would have packages of household items delivered to her door, taking every advantage of Amazon Prime and the UPS guy's muscles. She was worried about how she was going to pay the bills she was racking up, and knew that her paycheck wasn't even close to what she needed to pay her monthly expenses ... so she simply stopped checking her post office box. After all, she reasoned, she only cared about the packages, not the bills, and she wasn't ready to face her credit card statements head on.

Well, denial got her sick. She was unable to sleep most nights, and started relying on over-the-counter medications to try to get even a solid four hours. She was not eating well. Then, one day, she ended up doubled over in the bathroom at work with excruciating chest pains. Her coworkers, thinking she was having a heart attack, called 9-1-1. She was rushed to the hospital, where they kept her under observation for twenty-four hours. Her blood pressure was through the roof, and, although she hadn't had a heart attack, she *had* experienced a full-blown panic attack.

Finally, she had to face the reality of her situation. Her denial—and the stress it was causing—was actually killing her.

When we started working together, I could see that she needed more than just a budget. She needed a complete *LifeStyle Re-Design*—a plan for facing her financial demons, starting fresh, and creating her prosperity after divorce. And that's what we did. Today, she's well on her way to financial solvency, and feeling completely supported. No more panic attacks, no more avoiding her mailbox.

Each Theresa that showed up in my coaching practice left me thinking that, if I could help women look at their financial picture during and after their divorces as a gateway to true prosperity, wouldn't they feel more empowered about the new life they were creating? Wouldn't they be more likely to make decisions that supported their personal definition of prosperity, rather than avoiding and deflecting?

Out of that desire, my LifeStyle Re-Design Planning program was born.

I am blessed that so many women continue to bravely step into this vulnerable space with me as they start their journeys toward their prosperity after divorce. From their sharing and my work with them, I have created many tools under the LifeStyle Re-Design Planning umbrella, including my Divorce Support Programs and Money Day Spa programs, which help women sift, sort, learn, grow, and implement. In this book, I'll be sharing these tools with you so you create your own Big Shift like I did, and start working toward your personal definition of prosperity after divorce.

The Bottom Line

Imagine for just a minute that things really could be better. Imagine that you had a choice about what your life looked like. What would be different?

Well, it's not a fantasy. It really is up to you.

You get to choose how long you wish to sit in denial, resentment, anger, guilt, and shame. And, on the flip side, you get to choose and define what your "ideal life" looks like. When you are ready (and I imagine you are, since you're reading this book!) you can roll up your sleeves and dive into your very own LifeStyle Re-Design Planning.

In the rest of this book, we'll look at what it takes to create your redesigned life in six key areas—what I call the Six Pillars of LifeStyle Re-Design Planning: Financial, Emotional, Habits, Work, Family, and Spirituality. I'll take you through the very same process I used to create my own prosperity after divorce, and share many of the powerful, practical tools I use with my private clients. Through the lens of your relationship with money, success, and stuff, we'll dive into your current reality and map out a route to your ideal life.

I engaged fully with this process for over a year after I sold my business and gave myself the breathing room I needed to see my life clearly. It gave me a sense of empowerment that I'd never felt before. I set new goals for myself, created assessments and tracking tools to chart my progress, and started rebuilding. I created a "Prosperity After Divorce" vision board. I devoted my life to uncovering the paths that had been hidden from me for so long—the paths to my real, genuine prosperity.

The great news is, this process doesn't have to take you a year. You get the benefit of all of my experimentation, testing, and meandering; you'll also get the powerful lessons I learned from my own blunders, and the wisdom I've gained through working with my amazing clients.

You don't have to struggle through this process. All you need to do is come to the table with a willingness to see what's really happening in your life, and the desire to strengthen what works, scrap what doesn't, and start fresh on your own terms.

Are you ready to start your LifeStyle Re-Design Planning?

Part II

DESIGN THE
LIFE YOU WANT

WHAT IS LIFESTYLE
RE-DESIGN PLANNING?

I n the last three chapters, you've learned an awful lot about
me, my story, and how I was able to redesign my life to match
my vision of prosperity. You've also read some examples of
how my clients have been able to do the same in their own lives.
Maybe you've seen echoes of your own life in these narratives;
it's not for nothing that it's known as the "human experience."

In the next section of this book, I'm going to teach you my
exact methods for LifeStyle Re-Design Planning. Basically, I'm
going to give you the tools I use to create clear, actionable, trans-
formational plans for my clients every day—the same I used
to create my own transformation—and teach you how to apply
them to your life.

Are you ready to dive in?

So what, exactly, is LifeStyle Re-Design Planning? LifeStyle Re-Design Planning is just like it sounds: a strategy to redesign your life to better align with your current financial, emotional, habitual, work, family, and spiritual situation. Those six areas—the six Pillars of Prosperity—are the six areas of your life that affect, and are affected by, your finances and the ways in which you relate to money, wealth, spending, and saving.

But that's just the beginning. This process starts right where you are in this moment, but it also provides a road map to get you to where you want to be. It's like a GPS, guiding you to your personal vision of prosperity after divorce!

Especially if where you are right now isn't your prosperity ideal, you need a plan to move you out of your current situation and into something better. And, as you've learned so far in this book, you have to know where you are to see where you're going.

But, although the LifeStyle Re-Design Planning process starts with us gathering a clear picture of your current reality in the Financial Pillar, I actually want you to come into it from the other side: your dreams and goals around prosperity, and your vision of what you want your life to look like. Why? Because in order to get the most out of the work we're going to do together, you have to have a destination to plug into that prosperity GPS!

Your Top 3 Life Priorities

Goal setting is an integral part of this process. Right now, I want you to see your life as a blank canvas. You may be tempted to splatter your canvas with the red marks of your marital debt, attorney fees, and shared expenses for the kids.

But we're not talking about your baggage here; we're talking about your vision. This is your creation space, and it requires you to look forward, not back.

So, what does your prosperity look like? Paint a picture. Get out your notebook, and write about your prosperous life. What do you do every day? What do you have? Where do you live, work, and travel? But most importantly, how do you feel? What emotions are present in your prosperous life, and which rarely pop their heads in for a visit?

Let it flow. Don't worry about whether your vision of prosperity is "right" or "attainable." This is your *life* we're talking about; don't compromise your big dreams just to make them feel easier to get to.

When you're done, look at what you've written. Chances are, you'll see a couple of strong themes running through your vision for prosperity. Write down those themes. These are your top three priorities.

For example, travel, freedom, and abundance are my priorities. For you, creativity, stability, ease, relaxation, wealth, achievement, and helping others might be priorities. Pick your keywords carefully; you'll be referring back to them often as we progress through this work.

HOW TO GET THE MOST
OUT OF THIS WORK

Part II of this book is organized according to the six Pillars of Prosperity: Finances, Emotions, Habits, Work, Family, and Spirituality. Each chapter contains not only information about the Pillar, but also action steps and suggestions that you can put into play to flesh out your LifeStyle Re-Design Plan. (There are also worksheets in Part IV at the back of the book which correspond to the primary exercises described in these chapters.)

When you are starting this process, don't set too high a bar for yourself. Don't expect to do all of the exercises in a weekend, or change your financial reality in a week. Instead, make a commitment to work on a manageable portion of the exercises at a time. Maybe that means reading the entire section and then going back to do the exercises. Maybe it means completing one chapter per week until you have all six Pillars in hand to complete your Plan. However you choose to proceed, it's important to know that this isn't fluff work: you are creating the blueprint for a strong foundation for the rest of your life.

I compare this LifeStyle Re-Design Planning process to building a new house. When a builder is constructing a new building, they would never start with siding, windows, and a roof. They start with a strong foundation. They:

- Start with materials that are quality in nature. (Your quality materials are your emotional and spiritual temperature, your natural gifts and talents, and your willingness to create your prosperity after divorce.)

- Place the structural forms properly. (The budget you will create in the Financial Pillar represents the steel form that will hold it all together.)

- Allow the foundation to set and settle before the walls go up. This is a process, not a race!

Be Your Own Hero

I want to share one more tidbit with you before we move on to the first Pillar: when you start working with your finances in this way, and start to take charge of your life and budget in a way you may never have done before, you will become more than you have ever been. You will become your own hero.

As we discussed in Chapter Two, looking at your money issues will force you to face some of your darkest fears. But we grow through adversity—if we choose to. Think about your heroes in life. Chances are, they're people who went through some pretty dark times, and came out the other side with more joy, love, and excitement about life than ever before.

It's hard to see the light at the end of the tunnel when you're in the thick of your divorce, but you don't need to wait for someone to come along and pull you out of your adversity. You have the solutions you need right here in your hands, and inside yourself. All you need to do is commit to taking a step in the right direction.

Finding prosperity after divorce isn't impossible. All it takes is a clear vision and a willingness to do what it takes— *whatever* it takes—to create the life you dream about. And when you do it (as I know you will), you will be taking a stand for yourself and your dreams like never before.

If you can't picture this right now, don't worry; the steps you need to take, and the ways in which you can take a stand for your own prosperity will become clear to you as we move through the work in the six Pillars. For now, just know that this level of empowerment is coming, should you choose it—and that it's going to be amazing.

The Bottom Line

No matter who you are, what your current situation is, and where you want to go in your life, I know this LifeStyle Re-Design Planning process can—and will—work for you, as long as you are willing to look deeply, be brave, and stay committed. I'll be here with you every step of the way.

Ready? Let's start planning!

Chapter Four

FOR THE LOVE OF PIZZA, THINK IT THROUGH!

(The Financial Pillar, Part I)

Growing up, we always had what we needed—but not always what we wanted. We learned to be content with having less than what we considered ideal. However, once I was old enough to work, my contentment meter got reset. I realized that I wanted the finer things in life, and that—through hard work and a few lucky breaks—I could make more money than just what I needed to scrape by. I was able to purchase my first home at twenty-five, and my business before the age of thirty. After that, I could afford a bigger house, newer cars, nicer clothes, a private preschool for my daughter, and meals at fancy restaurants. I could even afford day care without flushing an entire paycheck down the toilet!

This lasted for fifteen years, the duration of my marriage. It seemed that the life we were living was more than full, and yet, my kids didn't have a mother who was home before eight o'clock at night. I was working ridiculous hours to furnish a lifestyle that wasn't truly supporting us. But, as usually happens when we get stuck in a status quo, I didn't notice what was really happening until I decided to leave—and a new financial reality hit me smack in the face.

It was my decision to divorce, so I thought it should fall on me to move out. Emptying the family home of half of our joint possessions felt like a bad idea. I didn't want to strip my kids' sense of security in the only home they'd ever known, so I left with just a couch, the Keurig, and a few duplicate kitchen tools. There was no moving van, no fleet of friends with pickup trucks; I was able to move all of my stuff—my clothes, shoes, books, and CDs, plus some extra things for the kids—in about five car loads.

What I didn't think about at the time was that, in order to fill a new house with even the most basic and necessary stuff, I was going to have to come up with a huge chunk of money. I needed a bedroom set and a dining room table. I needed beds, sheets, blankets, and pillows for both me and my kids. I needed a washer and dryer. If I ever wanted my kids to come and visit, I needed a television, and possibly a gaming console. I needed plates, cups, silverware, and coffee mugs. I needed a friggin' lawn mower. Every time I reached for something, I didn't have what I needed.

Stepping into my new place on Strawberry Street that first day felt like staring at a blank canvas. There was *nothing* in this house but bare walls and gleaming, empty floors. I was going to need a hell of a lot more than a couch to make this place feel like a home.

Over the next couple of weeks, I started keeping a running list of items I needed: things I would reach for automatically, only to find that they didn't exist yet in my new home. I was making trips to the store every other day to pick up batteries, kitchen gadgets, detergent, you name it.

Then, one day, I reached for my favorite cooking utensil, my Pampered Chef pizza stone, and … it wasn't there.

"Dammit! What was I thinking?" I asked myself aloud.

I had seasoned that stone to a dark, crisp brown over the last nine years. It was the perfect baking surface for any incarnation of pizza. And it was sitting in the drawer in my old kitchen.

Sure, I could buy a new one, but—as anyone who owns one of these pizza stones knows—the dark patina created through years of repeated use is what makes the stone so amazing. I valued this stone more than my Lenox crystal collection.

I had to ask for it back.

I figured the best option was an exchange. Like a nation hammering out a trade agreement with a hostile foreign power, I needed to come to the negotiating table with something to offer. I scoured the local tag sales that weekend and … *Voila!* A brand-new pizza stone in its original box, never opened. Grinning like a maniac, I called my ex to discuss the terms of the exchange.

His response? "*Hell*, no! That pizza stone is one of the best things in the kitchen!"

I started whining like a four-year-old, regurgitating a list of all the other things I'd left behind. I wasn't asking for the flat-screen TVs, the furniture, the chenille blanket, the Wii, or my designer towels. I'd even left the Christmas ornaments, for God's sake.

"Well," he countered. "You should have thought of that before you moved out."

Click.

Oh, no you don't, I thought. *This is war!*

I never did get that pizza stone back, although I tried like hell. Instead, I kept the new one I'd bought at the rummage sale. It's gained its own patina in the years since I moved out. It's not quite the same as the original, but it has its own history baked into it—the story of my new, re-designed life, post-divorce.

Before I moved out, one of my closest girlfriends (who had recently been through her own divorce) encouraged me to take a written inventory of *everything* in the house, including the contents of the basement, garage, pool house, and shed. Since I was not interested in stripping my house down to the bare walls, I brushed her off—but she kept pushing me.

"It's not about being vindictive. You need to do this because you'll want an idea of the value of what you're leaving behind when it comes time to do your financial affidavit."

In the end, I followed her advice, and I was glad I did. It made things a lot easier for my attorney and, although it didn't quite prepare me for the expense of setting up a new place, it did give me a basis for rebuilding. Turns out, most of the stuff I had didn't impact my life in any significant way, and I didn't miss it when it was gone. The things that were truly valuable—the pictures of the kids, my favorite CDs, the Christmas ornaments that my grandmother had given me (one a year until I turned eighteen), my scrapbooking supplies, and that friggin' pizza stone—*those* were what I actually needed to take with me. Unfortunately, I wasn't thinking too clearly when I made my list, and those things didn't end up in my car with the couch and the Keurig.

So please, learn from my mistakes. If you haven't moved out yet, do your inventory. There's a handy spreadsheet for you in Part IV at the back of the book! (If your ex is the one moving out, be sure to have a list of what's going with him.) Then, make a list of what you will need in your new place (or what you will need to replace when your ex leaves), and decide—within reason—what's essential, what's simply nice to have around, and what you can live without. Then, plan for your purchases.

And please, for the love of pizza ... take the damn stone.

THE COST OF STARTING OVER

The financial pillar of LifeStyle Re-Design is all about getting a handle on your assets and looking your current financial reality square in the eye. Part of that financial reality—and by extension, the prosperity you want to create—is your *stuff*: the stuff you own, the stuff you need, and the stuff you want to acquire. So that's where we'll begin.

If you've already gone through a transition in your living situation, you may relate to my pizza stone fiasco. If you're not there yet, this is a good lesson to remember: *stuff is only as valuable as the emotions and history you attach to it.* Be aware of what you're willing to let go and what you're committed to holding on to; then, make a plan, and do what you can.

We aren't always going to get everything we want in divorce, so you've got to pick your battles. I've heard of couples who have taken their fight over an inversion bench to court. Ditto for gourmet pans, the kids' swingset, and the king-sized bed.

Don't be one of those couples. Let's face it; unless an item truly is irreplaceable (like my grandma's Christmas ornaments), it's probably not worth going to war over.

That said, it's important to know what you're going to need to set yourself up in your new life, and stand up for yourself so you can get it. You'll want to know what stuff is essential, what is good to have, and what you won't actually miss. In order to make those decisions, you need to go back to your definition of prosperity.

If your definition of prosperity is "freedom," and you're considering a move cross-country because your kids are now grown and gone, you probably don't need a ton of heavy antique furniture weighing you down. If your definition of prosperity is "time," you'll want to keep your time-saving gadgets (like my beloved pizza stone), but not the ones that are going to sit on your counter collecting dust. And if your definition of prosperity is "financial stability," you'll want to make sure you do what it takes to keep your startup costs in a reasonable range.

But most of all, you'll want to have a plan.

I launched into my divorce without a plan—and my choice not to rock the boat cost me bigtime. Part of my definition of prosperity is financial solvency, but the choices I made in those first couple of months created a situation that put me further away from, not closer to, my goal.

With my salary, buying the stuff I needed wouldn't ordinarily have been a huge deal—but in addition to my "startup costs," I was also facing alimony payments, child support, and all the expenses for a huge house I wasn't even living in. This "fresh start" was not as fresh and liberating as I'd thought it was going to be. In fact, money was flowing out of my account so fast that I was starting to get scared.

Still, the only thing to do was get it done. I took advantage of every 30-percent-off sale at Kohls, and every 90-days-same-as-cash offer at Best Buy. I negotiated good deals on my furniture purchases. But even after frequent trips to Goodwill and raiding my mom's "double stash" of linens and kitchen items, it still cost me almost $10,000 to set up my new life.

After a couple of weeks, I realized that, although I'd thought I had figured out what my kids needed at our new home, we were still running back to the old house for this book, that pair of baseball pants, that curling iron, practically every day. My kids were definitely feeling the stress that came with moving every two days, and all of my admonishments to "think in advance" weren't solving the issue. When I pressed them, they'd respond with, "I didn't ask for this!"—which, of course, triggered my guilt mechanism. How could I expect my kids to think clearly when I was in a fog myself?

So, I decided the best option for all of us was to "double up" on the essentials that kept us running the marathon back and forth between houses. I purchased duplicates of my daughter's hair products, makeup, curling iron, hair dryer, and basic clothing items. My son got duplicate soccer pants, baseball uniforms, underwear, and socks. The only thing I didn't duplicate were their school books—and believe me, I tried. At the time, it seemed more important to me to lower our collective stress levels than to worry about the money—but all of this duplication cost more than $1,000.

I tuned it out. I simply didn't want to expend the mental energy to look at what I was spending, and whether it was a good idea.

In those early months, I was 100 percent in that space of emotional decision making. I was in survival mode, hunting and gathering what I thought I needed to rebuild my life and feel comfortable, secure, and prosperous again. I didn't consider the long-term implications; I just wanted me and the kids to feel supported—and, at the time, "support" felt like "stuff."

It took about six months before I really felt the financial impact of the move-out frenzy. At the beginning, I was so unsure about my financial future that I decided it would be easier to charge everything and pay for it later. "12 months at 0% APR" was music to my ears. It actually felt good (sad as it sounds) to be a "valued" customer of Chase Bank, Best Buy, and Macy's; I felt like leveraging my excellent credit gave me an upper hand, and gave me some breathing room while I focused on making sure my kids and I were going to be okay. It felt good to click "Buy Now" on my Amazon account so I could have yet another self-help book delivered to my door, or to enter my sixteen digits into Travelocity's payment screen so my kids and I could take a few days away.

Then, one hot Saturday morning in June, I sorted through the messy pile of mail on my counter, and … there was a bill due in full from Best Buy for $1,200, a bill from the furniture store for $2,800, a $1,000 bill from my attorney, and another $1,020 bill from Bob the Therapist because I was now three months over my free eight sessions and my insurance deductible hadn't yet been met.

My Chase Visa statement listed multiple dinners out which totaled $516, duplicate purchases for the kids in the amount of $508, and a Mother's Day spa day for me and my mom which cost $393 (not including tips). There were also charges for my new gym membership, yoga classes, our family day at Six Flags, and a $750 deposit for the vacation we were taking in July.

In total, I owed $8,296.99 in outstanding bills—and that was before rent, groceries, cable, or the electric bill. And *all* of it was due on the twenty-fifth of the month.

It was like being hit with a brick. For the first time in my working life, I would be unable to meet my financial obligations. I was devastated, ashamed, and totally panicked.

How could I have been so stupid? How could I not have seen this coming?

And, more, how had no one called me out on my spending rampage? I had an attorney, a therapist, a caring mom, a great group of friends … and in six months, not one of them had asked me, "Hey! Do you know what it's going to cost you to live on your own?" Not one of them said, "Didn't I just see you at Kohl's two nights ago?" or "Are you sure you can afford a vacation right now?" No one said a word.

I was so stressed that I thought about seeing Bob twice that week—and then promptly realized that I couldn't afford it. If I wanted to shift this, it was all on me.

BE THE (WO)MAN WITH A PLAN

Maybe my friends, family, and support network didn't speak up because they thought I really did have the money to do what I was doing. Maybe they thought it wasn't any of their business. Or maybe talking about money is still so taboo in our society that they were afraid to bring it up. Whatever the reason, though, I wished someone had brought my reckless-ness to my attention.

Well, what my network hadn't done, the bills had: my attention was once again front and center on my bank account.

What I realized was that I'd ended up here because *I had no plan*. No pen-to-paper budget. No consideration as to what was coming in, what was going out, or what was coming up. I had literally taken zero steps to figure out what it was going to take manage my new life with one income. In fact, the last proactive thing I'd done with regard to my money was to take that inventory of my household stuff—not that I'd done anything with the information beyond give it to my lawyer.

The thing was, I'd provided the main income in my house for years while my ex stayed home with the kids and did side gigs on weekends. It had never occurred to me that I might struggle financially now that I was on my own. But now, only six months after my move-out date, I was in over my head. There were so many new things to pay for—like my rented house, the kids' duplicates, extra gas for shuttling them back and forth, etc.— that my once-substantial cushion was now threadbare. Plus, my ex owed me more than $4,800 for his share of the kids' activities, school lunches, and medical expenses, and he wasn't paying up. Nor could I expect him to in the near future, since I didn't have $300 an hour lying around to sic my lawyer on him.

"I'd better start planning, or I'm screwed," I muttered.

The reality was, even though my paycheck and bonuses were the same as they had been before the divorce, I did not have as much income to throw around. No one coming out of a divorce does! I hadn't taken an in-depth look at my budget since we left the courtroom on D-Day. Now, six months later, I had an idea of what I wanted out of my new life—more travel, buying a house for myself, less work and more time with the kids—but no plan to make those things happen.

I needed to make some tough decisions about my spending *now*, so I could have what I wanted in the months and years to come. I had to rebuild my financial foundation so I wouldn't be shaken again like I had been when I saw those bills staring at me from the pile. My prosperity didn't look like working my butt off just to keep up with the bills. (I mean, at that point, I was working my butt off regardless, but at least I felt like it might be getting me somewhere!)

When you go from having everything you have built over the years to having a mere piece of that—whether it's 50 percent, 25 percent, or nothing—you have an opportunity amid the chaos: you get to choose what comes next. You have a clean slate on which to start rebuilding your foundation. You get to pursue what matters to you—your version of prosperity.

Your plan begins with looking at exactly where you are—at

the good *and* the bad. For the sake of your prosperity mindset, we'll start with the good—and hold onto it throughout.

The Good

When I talk about "seeing your reality clearly," that doesn't just mean looking at what's wrong and taking steps to fix it. It also means acknowledging the things you have, and using your gratitude for them as a tether to keep you from spiraling downward.

Things might not be perfect, but you *do* have a lot to be grateful for. You may not have all the stuff you're used to, but if you look hard enough, I promise that you'll find that you have more than you thought.

Long before I left my business and implemented my own LifeStyle Re-Design, I started taking steps to implement a daily "attitude of gratitude." I wrote down every bit of what I was grateful for on a daily basis, and tried not to focus on the things that had changed, or that felt like huge losses. I also kept a glass jar on the kitchen counter with little slips of paper beside it, where I encouraged the kids to write down one thing that they were grateful for that day; as the jar filled, we got to see our gratitudes growing.

Gratitude journaling is also a great way to keep track of your progress and successes, so changing your financial reality doesn't feel like a constant uphill battle. In the coming weeks and months, you're going to have to make some tough decisions about where and how to spend your money, and how you will set a solid foundation for the financial pillar of your prosperity. Focusing first on gratitude will make this easier—and maybe even fun.

The Bad

If you're struggling with the new cost of life after divorce, you're not alone.

Even if you're a Type A personality who always knows her bank balance, some things are just going to sneak up on you post-divorce. Maybe your ex is refusing to pay child support. Maybe your new rent is way higher than your previous mortgage. Maybe your kids need duplicates of everything like mine did. Whatever your situation, you have to expect the unexpected, and do your best to prepare for it so it doesn't hit you like the proverbial ton of bricks when the credit card bills come due.

Remember Anisa from Chapter Two? She had a steady job, and thought she would be able to manage on her own when she left her husband. But when her ex defaulted on child support, she still had to pay the additional home equity loan payment of $316 per month, a $215 per month minimum payment on their joint credit card debt (which, as you remember, she agreed to take on since she earned more), $376 per month for her student loan payment which could no longer be deferred, and $354 per month for the minimum monthly payment on the second credit card she'd had to start using to cover groceries, gas, and kids' stuff. Sure, she had a job and benefits, but her divorce was costing her an additional $1261 per month over and above her living expenses. She hadn't planned for this, and she was sinking fast even though she'd already cut her weekly retirement contributions to zero.

Without an additional $19,500 in yearly income, or some serious budget rearrangement, Anisa was not going to make it.

When she came to me, Anisa had been barely treading water for more than a year. She knew she had some serious money issues, but hadn't been able or willing to sit down and actually assess where she was and what she needed to change. Not only had she left behind her "pizza stone"—in the form of assets she could have used to supplement her monthly cash flow—she was in complete denial about her situation.

The good news is that almost nothing is irreversible. Once we sat down and actually got some clarity around where she was and what was happening, Anisa was able to get her feet back under her again and start making real progress toward her vision for prosperity. "It wasn't always easy to stick to the plan," she told me later, "but after about a year, when I looked back on how far I'd come and how much debt I'd paid off, I felt like Wonder Woman!"

The Pizza Stone Factor

Yup, everything comes back to pizza.

By now, you probably have started gathering some information about (or at least mulling over) your post-divorce financial picture. In Chapter Five, we're going to use that information to get super-clear on both your big-picture financial reality and the minutiae of your daily budget. But for now, I want to you leave the numbers out of the equation, and spend some time working through what you really *need* versus what you simply *want*.

I left most of the stuff I owned in my ex's house because I just wanted out. Some of that stuff—like a bed to sleep on, and pans to cook in—I needed. That stuff wasn't optional; it had to get replaced. But, looking back, I also spent thousands of dollars on stuff I just *wanted*—like the vacations, and the dinners out, and duplicates for the kids. Did that stuff make our lives easier? Sure. Was it absolutely necessary? No. If I had been thinking about the big picture of my finances with any clarity, I might not have dropped hundreds of dollars on duplicate sports gear and hair products.

For those first couple of months, I pulled out that credit card not just for everything I needed, but for practically everything I wanted. This created the illusion of security for me, emotionally, but it was backwards thinking. You can't lay the foundation for financial prosperity with a "fake it till you make it" approach. That will only land you further from where you want to be.

A real exploration of "want vs. need" requires serious, practical thinking, which is hard when you're in the middle of emotional upheaval. Still, it's necessary if you want to regain your financial footing and start creating your version of prosperity. So, I'm going to invite you to make a list on one side of a piece of paper of everything you need to have to survive. Then, in the opposite column, make a list of what you want— what you think will make you feel secure and prosperous—but that you don't necessarily need.

Your true needs have to be taken care of. You can't live without a bed, or food, or gas in your car. But your wants can wait, even if it doesn't feel that way emotionally. You can acquire them slowly, according to the plan and budget you create.

There is an exception to this, however. I call it the Pizza Stone Factor. There are some things that you can technically live without, but that give you so much pleasure and comfort that they feel like "needs." These could be things like photos and videos of your kids, heirloom holiday decorations, or your favorite snuggly winter blanket. When you're taking the inventory of your home, be sure to mark these items with a star, or circle them, so you don't forget to address them when it comes time to divvy up your possessions.

My ex and I only had one set of photos and videos of the kids. I made him copies of everything for Christmas the year after the divorce was finalized. It was a good solution to a problem that could have gotten ugly.

The Bottom Line

We've taken a lot of steps in this chapter to help you see your financial reality clearly, and get clear about your wants versus your needs.

Now it's time to dive even deeper, and put the magnifying glass on everything that impacts your prosperity, and start taking your power back, line item by line item.

Are you ready to budget?

Yeah, baby!

Chapter Five

THE BIG, BAD B-WORD

(The Financial Pillar, Part II)

One of the things that has made me so successful in business is that, when I don't know how to do something, I engage someone who does.

Somehow, though, I didn't realize that what works in business can also work in the rest of life. When I was going through my divorce, and in the months after our day in court, I didn't go looking for resources to support me. I didn't do my research so I would know what to expect from the various stages of grief, or engage people who had been there, done that so I could learn their tools for creating a new life after those papers were signed.

When my financial reality hit me in the face on that fateful Saturday in June, I realized that I had completely dropped the ball with this whole divorce thing. I hadn't employed any of my usual strategies. Instead, I plowed ahead blindly—and landed myself in a pile of debt.

Within a few days of my holy-crap-I'm-in-trouble Saturday, I watched an interview on *Today* while getting ready for an appointment. The interviewee was a woman who had just published a book about divorce. *Ooooh!* I thought. *I need to hear this!* I dropped my flat iron and grabbed my notebook so I could jot down her name and book title. Then, I opened my Amazon app and clicked "Buy Now" with record-setting speed.

That book was incredible for me on so many levels. I read the whole thing in one night. The author gave me a sense of hope about my new life. She hadn't wanted her divorce, but had accepted her situation—and, once she saw clearly what her new reality looked like, was able to create a life that was far better and more exciting than the one she'd left behind.

Sound familiar?

Yup, it's that "get a clear picture" thing again.

The one thing missing for me in that book was a discussion on finances. I went back to Amazon and searched for another book on the subject, but couldn't find anything. How was it possible that there were *no books* on how to deal with money in divorce?

Well, if no one was going to give me an easy way out, I had to create the solution for myself. I resorted to the basics: pen, paper, and calculator.

I understand money. I majored in business in college, and did well in accounting and economics classes. I had my Series 7 Securities license by the age of twenty-one. I had run a successful multi-million-dollar business of my own for nearly two decades. And yet, I really had to steel myself to face this whole budget thing.

I knew what I had to do: I had to figure out where I stood, create a plan, and hold myself accountable to it. I couldn't keep pretending everything was okay while at the same time allowing my money worries to keep me up at night. In other words, I had to re-design my financial life and lifestyle to fit my new reality, set some new goals, and decide what was really important to me and what was just thoughtless or habitual spending.

The first thing I had to do was get clear on what was coming in and what was going out so I wouldn't be upside down at the end of the month. At this point, I knew my fixed expenses each month: my rent and utilities; the phone, cable, and electric bills; my car payment; my divorce-related expenses. I also had a rough idea of what I was spending on groceries each week, and what I needed to budget for clothes for my growing kids so that they wouldn't be walking around in high-waters or too-small shoes. I knew Christmas happened in December, and that birthdays happened in June. I knew I wanted to keep saving for retirement and set aside some cash for my kids' college educations. I knew what I owed to my attorney, to Bob the Therapist, and on my credit card bills. But I couldn't help but feel that there was something I was missing.

I came up with a full list of monthly expenses, and a list of one-time expenses (like the attorney fees). Then, I got out a calendar and mapped out my upcoming big-ticket items— holidays, birthdays, school trips, oil deliveries, car taxes, sports costs, taxes, etc.—so I could see how much money I needed to have available at which points over the course of the year. Then, I compared these things against my monthly income.

What I realized was that, although I did in fact have the money to pay for everything that was necessary, I didn't have the money to go out to dinner with friends every night that my kids were with their dad. I *certainly* didn't have the money to keep picking up the tab for said friends, which is what I had been doing whenever someone was obliged to keep me company instead of hanging out at home with their own family. I *definitely* didn't have the money to take the kids on that vacation I'd been planning, or to splurge on the school party at the new paintball arena, or to pay entrance fees to Six Flags for my kids and five of their closest friends.

My initial gut reaction to this realization was sadness and guilt. I used to have the money for these things. Now, I had to deny myself and my kids because of the choice I'd made to end my relationship. I wallowed in that for a little while, but eventually I decided I simply had to face up to the fact that it was what it was, and I had what I had, and that was that. I had to start living within my means—my *new* means—if I wanted to create prosperity after divorce.

THE BIG, BAD B-WORD: BUDGET

When I was a kid, I would practice holding my breath underwater in my friends' pools. After a while, I could stay under there for more than a minute—long enough to freak out my mom—but eventually I would have to kick back to the surface.

I needed to take a breath and "reset" in order to keep going with my game. More, that breath was my *security*—the insurance that I wasn't going to drown. We all need to breathe to live. We can hold our breath for a while, and even pretend that we're mermaids and can live underwater forever—but eventually, we need to come back up for air, or we'll drown.

When we begin to work on our LifeStyle Re-Design Planning process, the first place to begin is with money, because money provides the most obvious piece of our security. You can't feel prosperous and secure when you are worried about your basic or daily needs. You can't feel prosperous and secure if you have no idea how to pay your bills on time, and don't have a system for doing so with ease.

The way I see it, you can live in one of three financial tiers:

- *Tier 1: Survival*, where you're doing whatever it takes to live day-to-day.

- *Tier 2: Status Quo*, where you're breaking even every month and meeting basic needs, but not really getting ahead.

- *Tier 3: Abundance*, where you've got more than enough cash flow to live the way you want to, with no financial worries.

Chances are, you want to be a Tier 3, but you're not there yet. (If you were at Tier 3 right now, you probably wouldn't have picked up this book!) So I'm going to assume that you're at a Tier 1 or 2 at this moment. Maybe you were at a Tier 3 pre-divorce, but now have been unexpectedly thrown down to a Tier 1 or 2, and are scrambling to adjust. Maybe you've always been a 2, and now are at a 1.

Whatever your reality is, it's okay. I've got your back. My work is to help you create a plan to get you from wherever you are now to that Tier 3 place of abundance, security, and the ability to live on your terms.

Knowledge is the heart of the Financial Pillar of your LifeStyle Re-Design plan. You need to know where you are and where you want to be so you can make a plan to get from here to there. As my story and the other stories I've shared in this book prove, what you don't know, or aren't willing to see, *can* come back to haunt you.

Thankfully, there is *always* a way out. You just have to be willing to make the climb.

So, before we dive into the logistics of budgeting and LifeStyle Re-Design financial planning, I want you to set aside any uncomfortable feelings you may be struggling with for just a moment, and think about the big picture.

Ask yourself: "Am I willing to do what it takes, right now, in order to create the prosperity I want?"

I'm assuming the answer is "yes," since you're still reading—so the next step is to create a tool that will take you from here to there. That tool is your *budget*.

Your budget is a living, breathing document that you will engage with every week, every month, and every year until you have reached your ideal level of financial prosperity. (And, by then, it will be so much a part of your daily life that you'll continue to use it until the end of time.) We will be creating your budget in this chapter using the very same exercises I developed for myself and my clients.

This is where LifeStyle Re-Design begins: with what comes in, and what goes out. Change one or both, and you'll change your life.

So, right now, I want you to start thinking about what we explored in Part I and the Part II Introduction. What are your Top 3 Life Priorities, and what do you need to do to start living them fully? These priorities will influence everything from your budget and money choices to the emotions, habits, and family routines that you cultivate. And they will be the basis of your motivation to get a plan in place! When we don't have clear goals, our motivation sinks and the things we do don't always sustain long term.

In addition to your top life priorities, I want you to think about your top financial priorities.

From the list below, choose your top three priorities. These will be the things you focus on in your budgeting as we move through the exercises in this chapter.

Your Top Financial Priorities

- Developing a money spending plan (budget)
- Personal debt elimination
- Establishing an emergency/opportunity savings fund
- Estate planning / wills and trusts
- Retirement planning / financial independence planning
- Investment planning
- Business cash flow and debt elimination
- Other _____

In the next section, we'll look at how money is coming into your life, and where it is going out, so we can gather an accurate picture of your financial reality. You'll use the exercises in this section to focus your investigation and compile all the facts. But first, let's talk about …

YOUR MONEY STORY

Everyone has a "money story." Really, it's the story of how we *relate* to money, not a story about money itself—but it has a huge impact on how we experience divorce (and any other upheaval or instability).

Your money story will determine whether you love budgeting or hate it, whether you're a saver or a spender, and whether you believe you can redesign your lifestyle using these budgeting tools, or you don't.

Right now, you're probably going deep into your money story. You might be telling yourself all kinds of things about why you can't or shouldn't make a budget, or why you can't or shouldn't be where you are financially right now. Maybe you're listing all the things you don't understand, or are scared of. Maybe you're digging your heels in, saying, "I can work this out without making your stupid lists." Maybe you're getting angry at me for even suggesting that you need to clean up your financial act.

It's cool. Everyone has their "money stuff." But if you want to get your prosperity on, changing your unhelpful money stories is a must. You can't get something different by doing what you've always done, and you can't write a new story by telling the same old yarn over and over.

As you'll remember from Chapter Two, fears about security, worthiness, and all kinds of other deep stuff show up when we talk about money. But if you allow your fear to keep you from looking at your money picture, your money habits, or your money plans, you will never change that story you've been telling about you and money.

Fear wants you to change nothing. Fear wants you to believe that you can't do this, and that you need to stay isolated and frightened. Fear wants you to be a victim to your divorce, your money situation, and your life in general. But if you don't want the rest of your days to be one long pity party, you're eventually going to need to face that fear down.

Love is the opposite of fear. Staring your money issues in the face and saying, "I'm going to do what it takes to create the life

I want to live" takes love—for your family, for your life, and for yourself. Love wants you to learn what you need to learn so you can step forward, not run away and hide with your old stories.

So if you're feeling the fear, get out your journal right now and rant for a while about how much this budgeting thing sucks and you don't want to do it … and then get another pen and a fresh sheet of paper, and come back to the table with me, so we can start falling in love with your budget.

YOUR BUDGET: WHAT YOU NEED TO KNOW

Most people dread the word "Budget" almost as much as they dread the word "diet." Whether they are making $30,000, $100,000 or even $500,000 a year, they envision budgeting as something that creates deprivation—something that puts restrictions on acquiring what they want. For many it even represents struggle or scarcity, and might bring back memories of their parents saying things like, "No, you can't have that. It's not in the budget."

Yuck. Who wants to budget when it feels like *that*?

But here's the thing: it doesn't *have* to feel like that! In fact, budgeting your dollars and your resources can be empowering. It can provide you with the ability to make choices based on reality, not fantasy. More, it will give you confidence in yourself and put you back in the driver's seat when it comes to your money.

The longer I work inside this money game, the more confident I am that your budget is the number one tool for you to create financial stability and consistency. Over and over again, I see clients create major life redesigns using budget alone. Once they embrace this new mindset of "I'm just telling my dollars where to go in advance," they quickly start to feel more empowered and in control. When an unexpected expense pops up, it's covered. Spontaneous purchases or emergencies, like car repairs, are handled without drama. They had budgeted their money to make purchases not only for the things they wanted, but the things they didn't even know they needed.

This can be you!

But first, get out your notebook or computer spreadsheet. It's time to get some real numbers on paper.

Your Basic Assessment

Step #1: Your Income

Use separate lines in your notebook or spreadsheet for each category of income.

> *Employment Income.* If you are working at a job, what do you take home per month (after taxes)? If your income fluctuates weekly, monthly, or seasonally, be sure to use your minimum income, not your maximum. Also consider that you will no longer be getting a "married" deduction on your taxes after you change your withholding status with your employer, so your take-home pay may decrease. (Don't forget this step: failing to change your withholding can leave you with a massive tax bill on April 15!)

> *Child support or spousal maintenance/alimony income.* Be sure to consider that, while child support is non-taxable, spousal maintenance/alimony payments *are* taxable. Be sure you are planning to have the proper amount set aside or paid in estimated taxes to avoid a big bill.

Other income. If you've got a side gig doing freelancing, housecleaning, tutoring, Uber/Lyft driving, network marketing, or anything else that brings in extra money, be sure that you're tracking it accordingly and delegating the proper amounts of taxes. As with your main income, estimate by the minimum amount you expect to make each month. If you are receiving commission, I would suggest not including those funds at all until they are actually received.

Step #2: Your Expenses

In this exercise, we'll chart out every penny that leaves your accounts each month. Be honest—and if you're not sure, estimate on the high end.

Child Support, Spousal Maintenance Payments and/or Property Settlement payments being paid to an ex-spouse. Spousal Maintenance payments are tax deductible, so talk to your tax professional for guidance in this area.

Housing Expenses. Mortgage payment/rent, insurance, taxes, utilities/heating (electric, gas, oil, wood, pellets, water), trash/recycling, internet, cable TV, phone, cell phones and data plans, home upkeep, repairs and maintenance, alarm services, and special projects.

Debt repayments. Note minimum payment amounts for all debts, including: credit cards, store cards, auto loans, personal loans, student loans, and loans from family and friends. (Note: If you want to pay more than your minimum payments, you can identify that amount once you have the full picture of your budget. For now, just write down what you *need* to pay.)

Seasonal purchases. Think about everything you do in your yard and how you decorate for each season/holiday. Include items like: lawn care services, pool opening/closing costs, pool maintenance, indoor and outdoor plants, starter plants and seeds, gardening supplies, mulch, snow removal services, outdoor decorations, and holiday decorations.

Transportation expenses. Car payments; gas, insurance; taxes; registration fees; license renewal fees; repairs and maintenance; AAA subscriptions; tolls; subway, bus, and train fares; Uber, Lyft, and taxi fees.

Food and household items. Groceries (estimate weekly on the high end), restaurant meals, coffee and tea, fast food and takeout, cleaning products and supplies, laundry supplies, paper goods.

Clothing and accessories. This segment is all about planning and what your budget can handle. Think seasonally and also about your needs vs. wants. Clean out your closet and consign things you no longer wear. (You can get some money back!) Set aside a fixed amount for "must-haves" and another amount for impulse spending.

Medical, dental, vision, and health. Health insurance (if it isn't already deducted from your paycheck); HSA funding; gym memberships; exercise classes and subscriptions; chiropractic care; physical therapy and other bodywork; acupuncture, energy work, and other holistic care; co-pays for doctors, specialists, therapists, etc.; vitamins and supplements; vision costs (glasses, contact lenses and supplies, etc.); dental expenses (cleanings, fillings, ortho-dontist visits).

Personal expenses. I like to see clients break these out instead of lumping them into their grocery costs, even if they're buying products at the supermarket. It's helpful to see what you're spending on personal care versus food. In this category, include: haircuts, color, and styling; shampoo, conditioner, body wash, and other shower products; facial care products; lotion, oils, and other body care products; shaving products; toothpaste, toothbrushes, mouthwash and floss; manicures and pedicures; other salon visits; non-medical massage and bodywork; facials and spa treatments.

Kids' expenses. Be certain to track these expenses separately from your own so you have records if you are contributing to or sharing these costs per the divorce agreement. Include: clothing, shoes, socks, underwear, and accessories (budget monthly if they are still growing, quarterly if they are not); diapers and diapering supplies; toys and games; sports, dance, martial arts, and other activity costs; sports, dance, martial arts, and other activity uniforms, gear, and travel fees; tuition costs; school lunches; day care and baby-sitters; after-school programs; field trips; summer camps and vacation camps; fundraisers; tutors; private lessons; religious education costs; and Halloween costumes.

Travel. Vacations (flights, hotels, food costs, and souvenirs), travel insurance, time share fees, retreats, and workshops.

Pets. Pet food; pet toys; collars, leashes, sweaters, and other gear; vet visits (routine and emergency); pet licenses and insurance; grooming; flea and tick treatments; and specialty treats.

Gifts. My best suggestion here is to make a list of all the people you buy for on a yearly basis. This includes: children, grandchildren, other family (siblings, aunts, uncles, nieces, nephews, etc.), friends, coworkers, kids' teachers and coaches, babysitters, other care providers (nurses, home care aides, etc.), and service providers (your hairdresser, esthetician, mail carrier, etc.). Then, after making your list of recipients, pull out your calendar and make a list of the occasions you buy for, like: birthdays, Christmas, Hanukkah, Easter, Passover, Valentine's Day, Halloween, Mother's Day, Father's Day, weddings and wedding showers, baby showers, housewarming parties, and kids' birthday parties. Most of my clients tell me that their gifting costs about $500 a year—when, in reality, it's more like $3,000! You will only know what your budget can sustain when you actually plug it in and do the math!

Charity/donations. Think seasonally as well here. Leave out payroll-deducted charitable giving as that is already subtracted from your monthly income, but include: tithing, monthly donations, adopting a family for the holidays, Go Fund Me donations, etc.

Miscellaneous. Include any expenses that don't fit into the above categories, like stamps, shipping costs, dry cleaning, office supplies (pens, paper, Post-its), planners and calendars, and books.

Savings. Include only items that are not deducted from your weekly paycheck, such as 401(k)/IRA contributions, whole life insurance, etc. Any other savings activity will be based on where you are in the 7 Baby Steps you'll learn in Step 3 of this exercise and how much you have to work with in your budget each month.

Step #3: Your Budget

It's time to do the math!

Get out your calculator, and add up all of the income categories. Next, add up all of the expense categories. Then subtract your total monthly expenses from your total monthly income. This will give you an idea of what you should have left after all expenses have been paid—or, where you're upside down.

Now, you need to decide what to do with the resulting total. If you have money left over, what can you do with it that will move you closer to your prosperity goals? If you're upside down, where can you cut back? (I suggest starting with your clothing, eating out, and personal care costs.) Do you need to earn, or find, extra money each month to move toward your goals?

You can approach this by looking at which Baby Step you are on.

Dave Ramsey's 7 Baby Steps to Financial Freedom

As you know, I'm trained to teach Dave's methods, and this is one of my favorites. I love the 7 Baby Steps because they're so approachable. They also give you a blueprint for where to put the extra money in your budget.

- Baby Step 1: Save $1,000 in an Emergency Fund

- Baby Step 2: Pay off all debt, starting with the lowest balance

- Baby Step 3: Create a real emergency fund equal to 3-6 months of expenses

- Baby Step 4: Invest 15 percent of your household income into Roth IRAs and pre-tax retirement

- Baby Step 5: Save for college funding

- Baby Step 6: Pay off mortgage early

- Baby Step 7: Build wealth, give, and live like no one else!

Let's say that you have $200 leftover each month, and you already have $1,000 in an emergency fund. You could spend that money on activities with the kids—or you could apply it to your credit card payments so your balance will go down that much faster. If your priority is getting through Step 2 (crushing the debt), then put that $200 against the smallest credit card balance. This process is called the Debt Snowball. Do this until all of the debts are paid and when they are, you will have that much more to both spend and save. This is your budget in action, and you can reassess the process each and every month!

The beauty of having a budget and working with the 7 Baby Steps is this: Let's say it's February, and you have a nice tax return of $1,788. You add that money to your monthly budget on the income side. Now, based upon which step you're working on, you will know exactly where to put that money! Maybe you can use it to pay off a credit card bill. Maybe it fleshes out your emergency fund. Maybe you apply it to your mortgage debt. But no matter where the money goes, you'll see the end result clearly, and feel your goals moving that much closer!

CREATE YOUR PLAN FOR FINANCIAL REBUILDING

Building a strong financial foundation starts with your budget, and because everyone's income and expenses are unique, your plan for rebuilding will also look different from anyone else's. However, there are some common strategies we can look at to get you started and heading in the right direction. These are:

- Follow the 7 Baby Steps

- Live within your means

- Plan for hidden expenses

- Make cash king

We've already talked about the 7 Baby Steps, so we'll move on to the next item, "live within your means."

Live Within Your Means

This strategy is exactly like it sounds. When you make your budget, make sure it's sound and accurate—and then stick to it religiously.

More, stop blaming or shaming yourself about your current means. Not having the money for dinners out with friends three nights a week does *not* make you a bad person. Nor does a negative balance in your checking account (although you'll want to adjust your budget if that happens more than once inside a month). Living within your means is about accepting where you are so you can get where you want to go, period.

As my mentor Dave Ramsey often says, "Live like no one else will, so you can live like no one else can."

Plan for Hidden Expenses

When we map out a budget, we tend to leave out things like gifts, kids' activities, random maintenance on your house and car ... and my favorite, those infamous girlfriend home parties.

Think about the last time you were invited to one of those parties. Your bestie probably said, "Just come and have some cheese and wine! You don't have to buy anything." And how much did you spend that night, once the wine went to your head and the saleslady did her shtick? How much cooking gear did you buy? How many pairs of super-soft leggings? How much peptide serum or nice-smelling body lotion?

I thought so. I can't seem to get out of one of those parties without dropping at least $100.

The same goes for kids' activities. Sports trips and new gear requirements always seem to sneak up on me—and trust me, some of that gear ain't cheap.

And don't even get me started on gifts: baby showers, wedding showers, birthday parties for my kids' friends, graduations ... Each time we get invited to a party, it's at least $25-$50. For weddings, it's more like $200—not including my outfit! Now, I *love* giving gifts. But a month that has two birthdays, a wedding, and a baby shower adds upward of $400 to my spending—and that money has to come from somewhere.

The lesson here: It's not wrong to indulge in this stuff if you have the extra cash. You just have to make sure it's in your budget so you don't end up short at the end of the month.

Random or irregular household expenses can also throw you

for a serious loop. Have you planned for annual maintenance like chimney cleaning, gutter cleaning, pest control, and lawn fertilization? If you have a pool or an irrigation system, have you budgeted for that? What about seasonal heating and cooling costs? Snow removal? Replacing that ancient hot water heater? When I sit down with women to look at these things, I often find an additional $2,500-$5,000 in home maintenance expenses that they hadn't budgeted for—and that ended up needing to be paid for with credit cards or the home equity line. Not cool.

Cash Is King

One of the best things you can do when you're redesigning your financial reality is to use cash for items that fall within your 'spending versus bills' categories.

Why? It's quite simple. When you use cash, you only spend what you have! But even more than that, there's something different and more immediate about cash. When cash leaves your hands you *feel* it leaving.

You know what I'm talking about. Remember that "quick stop" at TJ Maxx for "just one thing?" But once you're in the store, you pick up this, and that, and another thing—and by the time you get to the register, your "one thing" is a bunch of things totaling $61.78 instead of the $19.99 you planned to spend. Well, when you swipe your card, you don't immediately feel the impact of that $61.78. But when you whip out a Benjamin, and you only get $38.13 in change, you feel instantly that you've blown the budget. You get that "oh, shit" feeling right there at the register. You may even have second thoughts, and ask the cashier to remove one of those unnecessary items you snatched off the rack while waiting in line.

If you had put that $61.78 on a credit card, on the other hand, you wouldn't feel the impact of that purchase until thirty days later, when it—and all of the other "quick stops" you made that month—come due and you didn't budget the money to pay for them.

If you're not used to carrying cash, you're not alone. Most people have gotten out of the habit—to the delight of the credit card companies, who are raking it in by charging interest on everything you buy. Making the switch doesn't have to be hard, though. Here's how to do it:

On each payday, take out the exact amount of cash you have allotted in your budget for your spending categories. For example you should have clearly-budgeted amounts for groceries, household and/or personal care items, and gas for the car(s). If your budget allows, you can also fund envelopes for eating out, family entertainment, clothing, gifts, and even a miscellaneous envelope for things like stamps, dry cleaning, etc.

Separate the appropriate cash into your envelopes labeled for that respective category. If you prefer to do this virtually, you can use an envelope app on your phone!

For expenses that you won't be spending money on while out and about (i.e.: heating oil or car taxes) keep your cash at home in a locked safe, or in a separate bank account. I like the idea of moving those funds out of the "bill pay" checking so the money that you are accumulating sits elsewhere. But remember, this separate account is *not* savings or an emergency fund! This is you pre-planning for expenses that simply haven't arrived yet!

Spend your cash only on what you've budgeted for. Set a rule that you can't raid the other envelopes for extra funds. For example, if you spend $6 of your grocery money on coffee and a muffin, you need to buy $6 less in groceries, because your cash is gone.

When you first begin, (definitely the first month) keep your receipts in their respective envelopes so you can see what you're spending and where, and make modifications where necessary next month.

You'll be shocked how well this system works. I have clients who implemented what at first seemed like a totally tyrannical budget—but by the time the first month of "cash only spending" was over, they had money left over in every single one of their envelopes. If they beat the budgeted amount, they were then able to make a choice about adjusting the spending category downward and rebalancing the budget accordingly, or using the leftover cash to work on their current Baby Step. Either way, they were in total control of where those extra dollars went. How liberating can you get?

So, where do those extra dollars go?

I have a great calculator on my website where you can plug in your debt, APR, and monthly minimum payments to see how long it will take you to pay off the debt. Now, I want you to try this: go back and increase your monthly minimum payment by an extra $100 per month. You'll see that even a little bit of extra money has a significant impact.

The Bottom Line

While it's always possible that you'll end up where you want to be if you don't make a plan, it isn't probable, or even likely. That's why we do this work.

But the benefit goes beyond knowing what's in each of your

accounts and budget envelopes. When you do this work and get real about your life, you will be able to stop wishing for change and actually plan for it. Step by step, you'll see your prosperity being created right in front of your eyes—and what could be more empowering than that?

Now that you have your budget, it's time to dive into the remaining Pillars of Prosperity, starting with the biggest saboteur to your new budget plan: your emotions.

Chapter Six

AFGHANS AND HALF-FULL GLASSES

(The Emotional Pillar)

Just a few months before our divorce was final, I made a quick side trip to my old house to drop off my son's winter coat, which he had left at my place over the weekend. I knocked on the door of my former home (which was weird, but I was getting used to it), and heard my son yell, "Come in!"

I opened the door and walked in—only to see my son snuggled up on another woman's lap. The two of them were covered by my grandmother's handmade afghan, looking cozy as could be.

I knew my ex-husband had been dating someone else. I guess I just hadn't digested that this woman was actually going to become part of our lives—part of my children's lives. But there she was, snuggled up with my son under the afghan, on the same couch where the two of us used to snuggle all the time. I was shocked and furious and heartbroken all at the same time.

I managed to keep my composure, squeak out a pleasant hello, and tell my son, "You don't have to get up, honey. I'll just leave the coat here." Draping said coat over the nearest chair, I made a beeline for the door.

By the time I got to my car, tears were streaming down my face. Rationally, I knew I wasn't being replaced—but my heart hurt all the same.

As I drove away, I remembered a conversation I'd had a few years prior with my friend Bonnie. I was just starting to toy with the idea of leaving my marriage. I wasn't serious yet, just testing the waters.

"Really, Michelle?" Bonnie said. "You're thinking about leaving? Let me tell you how I see it. You have two contracts in your life right now: one with your kids, and one with your husband. The first one is a lifetime contract, no exceptions. The other you can break—but only after the kids are grown and gone."

I stared at her. Plenty of people I knew were divorced. Plus, the thought of waiting it out until my son was off to college made me feel like the walls were closing in.

Bonnie must have seen the expression on my face because she laughed, shook her head, and called the bartender over to order her second martini. "Want to know what's gonna happen if you leave? I'll tell you. You leave. Six months later, your ex-hubby decides to watch the football game at the bar down the road. Then, in walks Kat."

"Kat?" I knew a Kat, but I couldn't imagine her with my husband, unless … "Bonnie, do you know something I don't?"

"No, no. Just being hypothetical, love. Besides, *my* husband will end up with a 'Kaaaatherine.'" She drawled the name like a British socialite. "*Yours* will end up with a 'Kat.'"

"Oh. Um, okay." It was true. Prim and proper was *not* my husband's thing.

"Anyway, there he is at the bar, and in walks Kat. They have a couple of beers, and head outside to smoke a little weed. Just having fun, you know? At the end of the night, they go their separate ways. Then, the next week, when you have the kids again, off he goes to the bar—and wouldn't you know, there's Kat again. This time, they have a few beers and decide that it would be more fun to watch the game at your house. A few more beers, and she's spending the night ... in *your* bed. Eventually, the kids come home, and she goes back to her place for a while, but she really *likes* your husband, and she *loves* your really nice house, so she starts coming around more. Eventually, she meets the kids ... and she hates them."

"What? Who could hate my kids? That's stupid."

"Hey, some people just don't like kids, especially when they belong to the ex-wife. And when Kat eventually moves in, because she and your ex love each other, the kids will get the short end of the stick. Trust me, you don't want that."

I was speechless. It was a nightmare scenario, and it burned itself into my psyche.

Two and a half years later, driving away from my old house, crying my eyes out, still picturing my son snuggled up in that woman's lap, I wondered: what if this woman was my "Kat"?

I didn't sleep at all that night. I kept replaying what I'd seen, picking at the wound, examining all my fears. But as the night wore on, I started to soften, because the vision of my son with my ex's new girlfriend spoke louder than the story I was telling myself. She had been snuggled up with him, stroking his hair. Her other arm was around his shoulders, and he'd had a sweet smile on his face—one that said, "Maybe things are okay."

I realized that this new woman was not Bonnie's fictional

Kat. She really *did* like my kids. Instead of being defensive, she had been friendly and warm and kind to me when I entered what had once been my home. There had been understanding, not judgment, in her eyes. I hadn't handled it gracefully, exactly, but I hadn't yelled or raged, or insisted my ex come outside for a talk about how our kids weren't ready to meet his new crush.

Maybe, I told myself as I watched the sun rise through my bedroom window, having another adult around who would love and care for my kids was a plus. It would be difficult, but not untenable. Not a reason to blow up, or spiral into depression.

That said, I made extra-certain to show my kids a good time when they came over that week. There may even have been mention of a vacation. I had a sudden urge to remind them that I was fun and awesome, too.

YOUR EMOTIONAL THERMOMETER

What's your emotional temperature right now? And how is it affecting your prosperity?

Are you running hot, lashing out at everything, acting on impulse? Or are you frozen, unable to make changes or look at what's really happening?

Maybe you're feeling like some of my clients did when they first came to me to work on LifeStyle Re-Design Planning.

When Kara called me for the first time, she told me, "Tonight I heard some upsetting news. My soon-to-be-ex is trying to manipulate me. His goal is to break me—financially, mentally, and physically. He even told me that he would make sure I lose my job and end up face-down if I didn't give him what he wanted. In the four months since I left, I've learned to face many fears, but if I get served with a court order this week, I'll need all the help I can get."

Nancy, whose high school sweetheart left her after twenty-six years, said, "He was all I ever knew. Now, he has moved on and I have not. I have nothing to continue for; I just wake up every day, go to work, pay bills, and try to survive. I feel so discarded and unsure of how to 'un-wife' myself after so many years together."

We all like to think of ourselves as rational beings. But when emotions are running high and deep, we are much more likely to make irrational decisions, especially when we think a particular action will fill an emotional need.

Before my holy-crap moment and forced reset, I was definitely spending money in pursuit of an emotional goal. I wanted to make everything feel "normal" for my kids—hence the duplicates of everything. I wanted to prove that I could still support the lifestyle to which we were all accustomed. And a small part of me wanted to make sure that my kids knew that I was still the parent who could fulfill their need for love and support—the one they could turn to when things got tough. I was trying to counterbalance what I thought of as my desertion.

When I was forced to look at what I was actually doing—*why* I was spending so freely and uncharacteristically—it hurt. It made me feel small. No one wants to think their emotional needs have gotten the best of them, because we've all been taught that letting emotions rule you is a bad thing. But, as with every other Pillar in LifeStyle Re-Design, clarity is the key to dealing with your emotions as they relate to your prosperity. The more you deny the actions (financial and otherwise) that your emotions are driving, the longer you will stay stuck in your unhelpful patterns, and the more likely you are to undermine your own future prosperity.

Take my friend Brianna. In her ten-year marriage to an alcoholic, she spent a *lot* of money trying to buy a feeling of security. She had no savings, but a closet full of nice clothes and shoes. Fancy dinners out with friends were part of her weekly schedule. Being able to do what she wanted, when she wanted, gave her a feeling of control, stability, and value that she wasn't receiving at home. She deliberately avoided looking at her actual financial picture, because, "I was walking on eggshells every day trying to avoid an explosion from my ex. I couldn't stand adding the thought of being 'poor' to everything else that was happening."

Brianna and her ex never talked about money. Money was one of those things that could easily trigger him to seek solace in a drink, or ten—and, later, send his anger ricocheting around their home like a bullet. Brianna got so good at hiding their financial reality that, by the time the marriage ended, she had accumulated nearly $40,000 in debt. When she left, she took it all with her. Most of it was her doing, anyway, she reasoned, and it was better (and safer) to deal with credit card bills on her own than to start a fight with her ex over who owed what.

She was making good money as a freelance designer, but now Brianna was paying rent, a car loan, and massive credit card payments all on her own. Still, those new pressures didn't stop her from taking off to Europe for a month to "get her head on straight."

While she was away, Brianna didn't check her credit card balances. She didn't consider what it was costing her to run away from her reality. She was already in over her head—in the long run, what was a couple thousand more dollars? Yes, her adventure was healing in many ways ... but when she got home, her cold, hard reality came crashing in.

Then, a big contract vanished. Her steady stream of work

dried up. She had to borrow money for rent because her credit card minimums were over $1,200 a month. When her car blew a tire, she had no money to replace it, and had to borrow that, too.

Her core prosperity goals were freedom and security, but Brianna's avoidance of her financial reality actually undermined both of those things. She was desperate not to "feel poor," but she was basically a slave to her creditors, and her security was nonexistent because she didn't have a single dime in savings. She was living job to job, contract to contract, never knowing whether she'd have enough work that month to pay the bills.

Eventually, she had to declare bankruptcy to get out from under the mountain of debt she'd racked up. After her day in court, she felt like she could breathe for the first time in years. Like me as a child, she'd been pretending she was a mermaid— but she'd forgotten to come up for air.

CHANGING EMOTIONAL HABITS AROUND MONEY AND PROSPERITY

Changing emotional habits around money and prosperity can be challenging. In theory, all it takes is a choice—a firm decision not to do the things that undermine the future you want to create. In practice, it takes daily vigilance, willpower, and a keen awareness of the patterns into which you default when things get emotionally challenging. You need to monitor your emotional thermometer, and take steps to divert your course when you find yourself sliding into behaviors that undermine your vision for prosperity after divorce. If you don't do this— if you don't learn your triggers and take action to balance yourself when you get too "hot" or "cold"—you will repeat the same old patterns, and end up in the same old place, regardless of what you say you want your prosperity to look like.

Yup. Major reality check.

Right now, you're probably feeling some emotional pushback around what you've learned in the last two chapters—especially when it comes to your budget. So, be honest: what did the process of looking at your dollars-and-cents financial reality bring up for you? Did it make you angry? Did you want to blame someone—your ex, yourself, your parents for not teaching you about money, your friends for not having the guts to tell you that you were being an idiot, the postman for constantly delivering those stupid bills? Did you want to run away and hide in a hole until this all blows over? Or did it feel liberating, like finally taking a stand for yourself?

Now, I'm not a therapist. I'm a numbers girl. I don't want to make any claims that I can help you resolve your emotional crises; for that, you need time, tears, laughter, good friends, strong faith, and maybe your own version of Bob the Therapist. But I *will* tell you that your bottom line doesn't lie. And if you are brave enough to look closely, it will reveal a lot of what you've been hiding from yourself.

Cheryl was referred to me about a year ago by her therapist. After I shared with her how I started doing this work and what LifeStyle Re-Design Planning is all about, I asked her to tell me a little bit about what was happening in her world. Her words have stuck with me ever since.

"My divorce was a blessing, God knows. But I fall down all the time. I miss him, and then I don't. I remember the good times, and I feel crushed. Then, I remember the bad, and I stand up and dust myself off again. I've been trying to move forward, but these past two years have been a real struggle. Up, down, up, down ... I just can't seem to get my shit together! This emotional roller coaster is flowing over into every area of my life. Financially, it's like sitting in a boat with paddles by my side. I have what I need, but I haven't decided to pick up the paddles and row."

I know that everyone who's been through a divorce can relate to that on some level. For many of us, it's not losing the reality of the marriage that's hard; it's losing the story about what marriage is *supposed* to be. We're dealing with the loss of our expectations, our "shoulds," our fairy tale—and all of that plays into our money story and our prosperity journey.

One thing we women have going for us is that we know how to put words to our emotions. We are also usually pretty adept at knowing when our emotions are getting the best of us. The learning curve lies in learning not to let our emotional processing get in the way of our forward motion. This is true whether, like Cheryl, we are sitting in the boat with paddles by our side, paralyzed by fear and indecision—or whether we're tempted to drive that boat right over Niagara Falls because it was our ex's boat too, and there's no goddamn way we're going to let that bastard get away without paying for what he did.

So, how do we recognize the emotional triggers that set us off? How do we know, when we set out to go shopping, if we actually *need* a new pair of shoes, or if shoe shopping is simply a convenient, fun way to escape our feelings for a couple of hours? How do we stop ourselves from risking our financial stability for a few hours of emotional relief?

The first thing to realize is that 80 percent of our spending *is* emotional. In terms of pure survival, we actually need very little: basic shelter, nourishing food, and clothing to protect us from the weather. Everything else is driven by three things: convenience, comfort, and self-image. If we want to be and feel prosperous, chances are we want to achieve a certain standard of comfortable living. We not only want to surround ourselves with things that provide comfort and convenience, we want to see ourselves as prosperous, abundant, and successful. Sometimes, this leads us to live from the outside in, trying to buy an illusion of prosperity before we actually have the means to create real prosperity. This is emotionally-driven thinking, and it can be really damaging, not only to your bottom line, but to your sense of self in the long term.

The more you engage in wild emotional spending—and suffer the guilt, regret, and self-loathing that often sneak in once you get your purchases home—the less you will trust yourself. The less you trust yourself, the more you will fall victim to your harmful emotional patterns. It's a vicious cycle.

I could go on about this all day, but I think you get the picture. If you are in the process of divorcing, you *must* separate emotions from economics. The more frenzied your emotions, the longer your divorce proceedings, and the more costly your divorce. If your divorce is over, your emotional needs will still rule your finances until you figure out how to meet them positively and productively.

What Are You Really Feeling?

Many of the emotions that affect our spending before, during, and after divorce may have nothing to do with money at all. The heaviness of shame and guilt can knock us sideways when we least expect it. To alleviate these feelings, we tap into emotional and financial "coping" patterns.

For me, the hardest thing about divorcing was telling my kids that I was no longer going to be with their dad. The second hardest was telling my mom, who stuck it out in a challenging marriage of her own for decades before she found the good.

Breaking my promise of "forever" really hit me hard—and triggered me to play up my financial "competency" to make up for the fact that I couldn't hack it in my marriage. As I've shared, this led to overconfidence, overspending, and even more stress down the road.

Many women who come to me for financial guidance are in the same situation: trying to be all things to their family, financially and otherwise. Others carry tremendous blame and victimhood around their financial circumstances post-divorce. Either they are shouldering all the blame for their failed relationships, afraid to ask for what they need because they think the whole mess is their fault—or they are blaming their ex for everything, and feeling like they have no control over their lives because of their ex's actions.

These feelings are all natural and valid. They also have real consequences in terms of behavior, spending, and planning for the future. So whenever you catch yourself thinking, "I'll feel better after I go shopping," or, "I'll book a vacation to remind the kids that I still love them," or, "I can't think about the future right now; I just need to get through today," or "I can't believe he put me in this situation," check yourself. Ask, "Where is this feeling *really* coming from?" And then, find the resources you need to help you address the root of the problem—whether that's a new self-help book (from the library if your budget doesn't have room for book purchases!), a session with your therapist or coach, or a chat with a friend. Then, do what you need to do to change your ingrained behavior. When you do this, not only will you avoid digging yourself into a financial hole, you'll also feel empowered, stronger, and more in control.

Perhaps the best thing to remember when working on unraveling your financial and emotional entanglements is that rebuilding a life is *not* a one-woman job. It takes a village of support to create your prosperity after divorce, and get you back to your energetic, spirited, fun-loving self. (Remember that woman? You can find her again!) So don't be afraid to ask for help when you need it.

You have everything you need to create your prosperity after divorce already within your reach, because you have the brains, courage, and conviction to make it happen. All you have to do is pick up those oars and start rowing.

So, let's get started.

Working with Your Emotional Triggers

Unearthing your biggest emotional triggers takes more than just introspection. We need to look at dollars and cents, and review your spending over the last several months. When we do this, we'll gain an understanding of which of your purchases were emotional or spontaneous, and which were planned and necessary. This is great information to have, because awareness is half the battle.

Start by looking at your purchases over the last thirty days. Gather your receipts, or spread out your credit card bills and bank statements. Consider each purchase, and what motivated you to make it. Compare your feelings to the list of emotional spending triggers below, and see if any ring true.

Be brutally honest here. No one likes to think that they're engaging in these behaviors, but we all do so to one extent or another. It's not "wrong," "bad," or "stupid" to succumb to emotional triggers. It's just not helpful in the long term. So let the past be past for now, and look at what you can choose right now to start creating your prosperity after divorce.

Common Emotional Spending Triggers

Feeling judged, less than, or overlooked >>> Keeping up with the Joneses and protecting your image. If you feel like you're "less than" others, and care deeply what others think of you, you might spend too much on things like designer clothes, bags, and sunglasses; buy or rent a house that's beyond your means; or splurge on lavish vacations you can't afford just to prove to others that you can.

Feeling fearful or uncertain about the future >>> Spending it all. You may find that you spend money just because you can—because "you only live once." A raise or unexpected income immediately goes to spontaneous and unnecessary purchases. You have trouble saving. When you review the month, it's not what you buy that's the issue, but the fact that you always spend money as soon as it's available. Ask yourself if you fear that money will stop coming in. Often, that's why we buy everything we "need" all at once instead of planning and saving.

Wanting to numb challenging emotions >>> Spending binges. Shopping sprees are like binge eating: they take away the pain in the moment, but bring it back tenfold later on. Many of us get an emotional kick out of spending. We say, "It just makes me feel better"—meaning, it distracts us from feeling bad for a little while. We buy because it "feels right" and then question the purchase when we come down from our high, most often before the credit card bill even arrives in the mail.

Avoiding painful emotions, wanting everything to be perfect >>> The need for immediate gratification. We live in a "right now" world. We carry our computers in our hands, get news via text instead of on the six o'clock broadcast, and have access to instant credit twenty-four hours a day.

When we see something that we think will satisfy one of our emotional needs, we want it *right now*. There is no need to pause and assess when you can whip out your credit card now and think about it later.

The desire to protect your standard of living, fear of change >>> "Status quo" purchases. Unless you're intentionally trying to simplify your life, you'll assume that any expenses incurred protecting that lifestyle are necessary. But divorce clearly causes an immediate change in income and family status that may suggest—or require—a different, more modest standard of living. Purchases made just "because I've always done that" are a telltale sign.

The need to overcome past problems >>> Habitual or excessive spending. If you were materially deprived at some point in your life, it's natural to want to avoid repeating those times. For example, maybe you buy a Starbucks latte every day at work because your ex tried to control your spending and threw a fit every time you didn't make your coffee at home. In this case, your newfound freedom to spend what you want may feel like a fun middle finger salute to your ex. Or, maybe the source is further back in your past. Maybe your parents were poor, and you've promised yourself you would never need to sacrifice like they did, and so you refuse to give up the things that spell "success" to you even when they're no longer in the budget.

Wavering self-worth >>> "I deserve it" purchases. When I sat down to assess my emotional spending, I had many "I deserve it" line items on my list of purchases. Often, these are items that are self-centered (think manicures, fancy jewelry, salon visits, personal care items, and those deadly shoes). If you find yourself saying, "But I *deserved* a day at the spa" to justify a $500 splurge, you're probably dealing with this trigger.

In reviewing your past several months of purchases, do you notice any of these triggers in your spending habits? Maybe you recognize the result—like the "I deserve it" purchase, or the desire to protect your standard of living—but don't know how to address the underlying psychology. This is when you turn to your emotional resources (like Bob the Therapist or your smarty-pants best friend) for help. Whatever is causing you to act on these triggers, you need to deal with the root cause. If you don't, it's unlikely that you will ever learn to control your spending and make the changes necessary to create true prosperity according to your definition.

I know it's hard to hold up that mirror to your own behaviors and feelings, but don't be afraid to confront those emotional triggers whenever you find them. Often, once you know they exist and actually look at them (instead of ignoring or avoiding them), the solutions you need to overcome them will show up. In any case, it's a battle that's worth fighting.

How the LifeStyle Re-Design Planning Budget Helps with Emotional Spending

When you don't have a plan, spending just ... happens. Money comes in and goes out, in all different directions. There's no flow toward a goal.

Many clients come to me with a very clear pattern of emotional spending. When I work out a LifeStyle Re-Design Plan for clients, it is based upon a template. First, we ensure that their basic needs are going to be met. Then, I help them develop a strategy to achieve their goals, and at the same time counteract the emotional spending triggers that undermine those goals.

For example, if a client's goal is to pay off $10,000 of credit card debt, adding in emotionally-driven "I deserve it" purchases will slow or negate her efforts to pay down those balances. So, instead of simply making her spending "wrong" or "bad" (which may actually make her underlying self-esteem issues worse), we have to come up with a different way for her to feel cared for and validated that doesn't cost hundreds of dollars per month.

With LifeStyle Re-Design Planning, everything is clear. That's the reason why it works so well. I help clients allocate dollars and cents to various categories in their budget so they can see where their true priorities lie and watch positive progress happen every single month. But as you probably found if you did the exercises in the previous chapter, budgeting doesn't have to mean living on a shoestring. If nice clothes are a priority, we build in a clothing budget—a set amount of money that can be freely spent on clothes each month, without guilt. I've even found a cool Virtual Envelope app where clients can see, in real time on their phones or computers, the amount of money left in each spending category.

It's hyper-empowering to know that you have an envelope to pull from for things like auto repairs and other emergencies that you'd never previously budgeted for. It's just as empowering to plan for your "fun" spending, and actually enjoy your shopping trips without the surge of guilt on the drive home.

After working with me for several months, my client Joy shared with me her new outlook on life.

"I didn't really want the divorce, but here I am. Some days are tougher than others, but I have a handful of really supportive friends, and two awesome daughters to help me through the rough patches—and I have you! Thank you for walking with me as I regain my legs. Having a vision of my financial picture and setting new goals around my finances keeps me feeling like I'm taking some control. It's also led me to try new things because I now have enough in my budget to do them. They are not extravagant, but they are so exciting. I had never driven more than an hour from our home, but this summer, I drove cross-country to bring my daughter back to college and we had a blast. It was a true adventure, and I enjoyed every mile of my return trip—even stopping to eat in restaurants by myself! I have now joined a hiking group through Meetup.com (thanks for the suggestion) and am venturing out each weekend, seeing new places, meeting new people and finding my mojo. Losing a marriage and a child to college all in the same year felt so overwhelming but thanks to your LifeStyle Re-Design Planning and my own hard work, I'm finding my way."

Bailey told me, "I realized that if I had the courage to look at the super-emotional financial stuff, I could muster up the courage to deal with the rest of my emotions as well. Working with you helped me heal in other areas because I had such a positive experience in this one!"

And Amandine shared, "I went from the pits of despair to the heights of knowing and experiencing total peace around money."

And that, my friend, sums up why this work in the Emotional Pillar is so important. The divide between the depths of despair and the heights of peace *can* be bridged when you're willing to take a stand for your own future prosperity and happiness, process your emotions around money proactively, and change the behaviors that no longer serve you.

Emotional healing around money (or in any area of life) doesn't happen overnight. It takes practice and perseverance to change habits that were years, even decades, in the making. But it can be done—I've seen it over and over. The key is to be firm but gentle with yourself. Be aware that you will trip up from time to time, but don't let *tripping up* become an excuse for *giving up.*

We all trip up from time to time. It happened to me just this past summer. I had a super-busy couple of weeks and I just stopped tracking my spending. The first day, I knew I was slipping. The second day, I knew it, too. By the third, I figured I was fine, and I would just add up my receipts over the weekend. Then, before I knew it, two weeks had gone by, and I had a purse full of crumpled receipts that I needed to tally.

By the time I finally got my crap in order, I found out that I had overspent my "dining out" envelope by $211! I remember looking at the app on my phone about halfway through that two-week period and seeing that my balance in that envelope was only $38.19, but I ignored it and kept spending, thinking, "I have extra in my grocery envelope since we're not eating at home, so it will all even out." Well, it didn't exactly work out that way. When I was done figuring, I had depleted not only my dining out envelope, but my grocery envelope *and* my play money envelope. Oops!

The great thing about this, though, was that I was able to immediately reset myself and shift my behavior to get back on track. I reminded myself of my plan, my vision for the future, and the reasons my budget was in place, and started over.

None of us are perfect. We all make mistakes—sometimes big ones. But having a solid understanding of how we relate, emotionally and behaviorally, to money, security, and prosperity can help us plan for the bumps in the road, and give us the clarity we need to change our behaviors so we don't keep making the *same* big mistakes over and over.

CENTERING IN THE EMOTIONAL PILLAR

Because I work through the lens of money, much of my work tends to be practical in nature. I help my clients come up with plans—aka, budgets, goals, and future visions—and then execute them in real life.

But I also understand that, when we're dealing with something as big and emotionally challenging as divorce, we can't always just say yes and dive in. Especially when it comes to our emotions, we have to work through some pretty complex stuff to get to a place where we feel ready to embrace our new life.

Because I'm not a therapist, I don't want to give you any pointers on the best way to deal with your emotional challenges; only you can know what path is best for you. I can, however, give you some examples that have worked for me and my clients to clear negative or stuck emotions, alleviate feelings of apathy, sadness, and hopelessness, and if any of these ideas appeal to you, road-test them yourself to see if they help. Used in conjunction with your budgeting process, they can go a long way toward empowering you to pursue, and create, your version of prosperity in your new life post-divorce.

Michelle's Emotional Re-Design Action Steps

- *Find a good therapist.* Seriously, it's so necessary to have an impartial, caring professional to help you clear out all the emotional gunk.

- *Create a vision statement for your life after divorce.* If you don't know what you want, you won't ever know what to do. Write a sentence or two about the general ways in which you want to approach and engage with life, including financially. Memorize it or post it somewhere you can see it every day, and repeat it often.

- *Create a vision board as an extension of your vision statement.* Using pictures, words, and abstracts, create a vision of what you want your new life to look and feel like.

- *Journal.* A lot.

- *Complete the Emotional Trigger exercise* from the previous section, reviewing the last 30-60 days of purchases to ferret out emotional spending habits.

- *Join a support group, online or in-person.* * Engage in workshops, retreats, classes, or other learning journeys that appeal to you and help you move forward. (Just be sure to budget for them!)

THE HALF-FULL GLASS

Over the years, my close friends have asked me numerous times to "just cut it out with the glass-half-full sermons, already!"

I've always been a glass-half-full kind of girl. I never knew how to just listen and let my girlfriends vent; I always felt that you could turn any frown upside down if you had the right perspective, and doled out unsolicited advice accordingly.

---

* Check out my "Prosperity After Divorce for Women" private Facebook group at Facebook.com/groups/ProsperityAfterDivorce

Then, I got divorced—and suddenly, there I was, three-quarters empty, tired, and defeated.

Thankfully, none of my friends tried to exact revenge with pep talks of their own. When you're in that place, I realized, nothing outside of you can pull you out of it. It has to be an inside job—and if you're feeling like a victim, or just resisting whatever you need to change, all the platitudes about "looking on the bright side" will only piss you off.

I've been a student of the Law of Attraction since my early twenties, but during my divorce, my practice and belief stopped dead in its tracks. Waves of negativity would wash over me daily, and I felt like there wasn't a damned thing I could do about it. Chocolate, ice cream, and Comedy Central all failed to pull me out of my rut. I walked in and out of this state of negativity for more months than a bear hibernates. My meditation corner was full of dust bunnies, there were dirty clothes tossed on my "thinking chair," and my scented candles hadn't been lit in so long that they'd started to lose their smell.

Part of me knew that this was a "transition state," but it was *so* not where I wanted to be. It took me six months to realize that this new, glass-half-empty version of me wasn't going to slink away to die on her own. It took me several more months to accept that this emotional area was going to be the biggest area of growth for me. It had been easy to stay positive and peppy when everything was going according to plan—but now, I had to put everything I'd learned over the last fifteen-plus years to the test.

Almost daily, I asked myself, "How do people stay positive in the face of adversity, hardship, trauma, and transition? Why does this feel more difficult now than it did before?" As I started to ask these kinds of questions, the truth quickly became clear: I was the one keeping myself in a negative space.

I had to *choose* to practice positive thinking, compassion, and happiness if I wanted those things to be part of my daily life. They wouldn't just happen automatically, according to some specific set of circumstances.

I wanted to smack myself upside the head. "Duh!" Of course I'd always known that my happiness was a choice—it was one of the first things I'd learned when I started researching the Law of Attraction—but, as I discovered, knowing it intellectually is *way* different than practicing it in real life.

My next realization was that, if I wanted to practice positive thinking, I needed to make time for the things that helped me feel positive: prayer, meditation, and reflection through journaling. I started building these things into my day, even if it meant getting only four and a half hours of sleep instead of five. I also made time before bed for reading inspirational books and listening to podcasts and audiobooks.

One of the most important things I learned during this time came from Abraham, channeled by Esther Hicks. It's called the Emotional Guidance Scale. Basically, it's an emotional barometer, with feelings like anger, depression, and apathy at the bottom, and joy, elation, and unconditional love at the top. The premise of this is that we are always on an emotional continuum, and we don't have to move from one end of the spectrum to the other in order to create a shift in our emotional frequency. For example, if I was feeling angry, I didn't have to rocket up to "pure joy" in five minutes; I just had to shift my thoughts enough to move myself from "anger" to "frustration" or "irritation" in order to feel lighter and more able to face my day. Of course, I would have loved to move myself from "anger" to "joy," but honestly, in the midst of the divorce, that was simply too much to ask of myself. Moving from empty to just under the half-full mark, however, was doable, so that's where I started.

The bonus to this was that, whenever I worked to "fill up" my glass and ease out of negative emotions, I inevitably found a pattern around my emotional or financial behavior that needed to be shifted.

The Bottom Line

Your emotions are amazing. Not only will they tell you what's happening inside you, they'll point blazing arrows at the patterns in your life that need to change—including patterns around your relationship to money.

Now that you have more understanding around why and how your emotions influence your spending, how do you feel? Excited? Afraid? Frustrated? A little of all three? Don't worry: all of these are totally normal. Just don't let these new feelings, on top of all the old ones, get in the way of the commitments you've made to yourself in the form of your budget. Just because you feel something doesn't mean you have to act on it. Instead, you can honor your feelings, get to the root of what's driving your behavior, and choose a different action—one that will move you toward a healthier, more prosperous place.

If the information in this chapter resonated with you, but you aren't sure how to put it to work, reach out for help. Get the professional support you need to move yourself into a place where your emotions aren't pushing you into a downward spiral, or away from your prosperity. I can't say it enough: you don't have to do this alone.

So, take my hand, and let's move into the sister Pillar of your emotions: the Habits Pillar.

Chapter Seven

DUMPED BY A
TALK SHOW HOST

(The Habits Pillar)

In November of 2009, just as I was getting my bearings post-divorce and feeling as though my journey was becoming less rocky, Oprah announced her retirement.

"What?" I spluttered at the TV. "*Now?* You have *got* to be kidding me!"

You may be thinking, *So what? Big deal!* But it *was* a big deal to me at the time. I had finally figured out how to unwind when I didn't have the kids, and part of that routine was watching DVR'd episodes of *Oprah*. From the screen, she encouraged me to master my life purpose, embrace adversity, and search for the lesson in everything. She taught me how to talk to my children about sex, why meditation is so important, and how spirituality and God can be separate or the same for different people.

Oprah was my life coach, my inspiration ... and now, she was *retiring*? My world was rocked.

It may seem strange that a TV show was such a huge support mechanism for me, but Oprah had a magic about her. The content she shared was important and interesting, yes, but the biggest benefit of spending time with her was that she reminded me that *I was not alone*. Each evening as she brought me into her space, I felt like I was surrounded by other women who were just as vulnerable as me. All of us were showing up to learn how to be better mothers, wives, daughters, friends, and people, together. I felt that I was part of a strong community—one where I didn't have to wear a name tag, or do anything except be myself and grow as a person. Sometimes, I felt more connected to the people in Oprah's circle than I did to the people at the networking events and PTO meetings I went to.

As I contemplated what the end of Oprah's run would mean, I remembered the time in 1983 when *M*A*S*H was airing its last episode. My parents made tee shirts and an honorary cake, and invited their closest friends to their "*M*A*S*H Farewell Party." They all watched this piece of history together, shed some tears, and shared memories about their favorite characters and episodes.

I muttered to myself, "No *way* will I be hosting an Oprah party." Not me. I was too pissed off. I had a bucket list of items that I had not yet achieved, and being part of her audience alongside my mom was one of those dreams. In 2004, I had plastered a picture of Oprah drinking a glass of champagne at her fiftieth birthday bash onto my dream board, and made sharing her space a goal. So, not only was she messing up my evening habits with her silly retirement crap, she was tearing up my dreams, making me question my belief that the Universe could, and would, manifest my desires once I asked for them.

This was *not good*!

I never was, and never will be, a rerun girl, so I had to figure this out ASAP so I could fill this DVR time zone that would suddenly be empty. *Grey's Anatomy* was entering rerun season, so that wasn't an option. What else could I watch to unwind on my non-kiddo nights?

Then, it hit me. I didn't have to watch anything. I was only searching for TV shows because my habit was watching TV at this time. I could actually fill this time with *anything I wanted.*

I'd always wanted to have time for exercise. I never fit workouts into my schedule because there were always other "more important" things to do—work, school projects with the kids, networking events, employee reviews, client meetings, kids sports leagues, grocery shopping ... blah, blah, blah. I envied women who worked out every day like it was as easy as taking a shower or brushing their teeth. Why did *they* have time to take care of themselves, but I never did? (Actually, envy might be too nice a word. I despised those women.)

Well, I never had the time because I had been filling it with other things. But here I was, with one whole, shiny hour that was no longer committed to *Oprah*. If I really desired health—and I did; it was on my dream board, right next to Oprah and her champagne—why not use this time to get healthy?

There was *power* in that one hour a day. I could claim it, all for myself.

So, I dusted off my ten-year-old Lifecycle bike (which, of course, was still in mint condition, having been used only a few times), asked my new man to help me hang my heavy bag from the basement ceiling, and dug out my old cardio kickboxing gloves. These were my new companions for the Oprah Hour.

I worked out just four hours a week—on the nights I didn't have the kids—but within a month, I was feeling stronger and more energetic. If I had a negative day, I beat on the heavy bag. If I had a mediocre day, I rode the bike. Within four months, I had dropped two sizes and twenty-two pounds.

I could have just changed the channel and found another show. I chose instead to think outside the box and take my time back.

And guess what? I had Oprah to thank.

HABITS MAKE OR BREAK YOUR PROSPERITY

We are creatures of habit.

I didn't fully appreciate this until my "Oprah moment"—but after that day, I started seeing unconscious habits and patterns of behavior in every corner of my life, including my finances.

When I sat down to chart out my budget, it was super-easy for me to write in my normal bills with their attendant due dates. Of course, some of them (like the electric bill) were going to fluctuate month to month, but for the most part things like my rent, the mortgage on the big house, life insurance, car insurance, and the cell phone bill were consistent from month to month, so that part of my "expense" column was pretty solid. What *wasn't* solid were my weekly living costs: groceries, eating out, greeting cards, last-minute presents for my kids' friends' birthday parties whose invitations I'd dug out of piles of school papers, and the kids hitting me up for cash to go out with their friends. These things always added up to more than I thought they should.

Then, there were my ... um ... *habits*.

It was very clear to me when I looked at my Financial Pillar that I should have more money left at the end of every month than I did—even accounting for those darned last-minute birthday parties. It was also clear to me after I sat down to review ninety days of credit card statements that my Chase Visa points weren't multiplying all on their own. My habits were costing me hundreds of dollars every month.

In those transactions lists in my online banking portal, I could see my morning dash out the door and the seductive call of the Dunkin' Donuts drive-thru. I didn't *need* to stop for coffee: my Keurig was one of my two prized divorce possessions. I also had a brand-new, four-slice toaster sitting on my countertop that was perfectly capable of crisping up my favorite onion bagels. I wasn't hitting the Double D because I had to, or even because I wanted to. I'd simply pulled into that drive-thru enough times that it had become a habit; an unconscious part of my morning routine.

Just for fun, I added up thirty days of Dunkin' Donuts visits. They totaled $247.90.

"Holy shit!" I said to myself. "That's a car payment!"

Then, I multiplied it by twelve months: $2,974.80. I was spending nearly *three thousand dollars a year* on coffee and bagels.

On a roll now, I printed out ninety days of statements and started adding up the other habitual spending I saw. There were line items from Panera Bread, Ruby Tuesday, Chili's, our favorite sushi and Hibachi spot, and a dozen more. My early morning, mid-day, and evening pit stops took up ten times more space on the page than necessities like gas for my car. My eating-out habit, which consisted of both lunches at work and dinners with or without the kids, had cost me $918.13 in just the last thirty days.

"Do it, Michelle," my inner grown-up said. "Multiply it by twelve!" Holding my breath, I did. The numbers on my little handheld calculator screamed at me: $11,017.56.

I couldn't breathe. Those two categories alone—eating out and morning drive-thru stops—totaled $13,992.36. Multiply that by 4.9 (the number of years it would take to settle out with my ex) and that total rose to $68,562.56!

That was insane.

Internally, I rationalized that the month I'd just studied was worse than usual because we'd done a bunch of school shopping and evening sports practices were in full swing. I'd also had quite a few early morning meetings on the days when the kids were with their dad, so of course I hadn't had time to prep anything. Then, there were the two weekend tournaments that kept us on the field from 8:30 a.m. until 6:00 p.m., so I didn't have time to do the grocery shopping ...

But, of course, the other two months were just as bad.

My inner teenager screamed, not wanting to face the music. "Really? Do you not see my Superwoman cape? I'm doing my best here!" (Okay, I may have even launched into the "But I'm a single mom and a business owner" backup speech I saved for really special occasions.)

Annoyed, I pushed back from the dining room table, swept up my imaginary cape, and went into the kitchen to make a coffee. However, instead of validating the existence of the Keurig by actually using it, as I had intended, I reached for a wine glass and the half-empty bottle of Riesling in the fridge. Blue bottle in hand, I slunk back to the table. I had to finish this.

It wasn't just about cutting my spending. I had uncovered some hidden traps I hadn't even known existed. I had to keep digging in order to know not only where I was spending my money, but why. Then, I could make a plan to change what wasn't working.

The longer I sat there tallying the numbers on my mini-calc, the clearer the picture became. I wanted—no, *needed*—to get back in the driver's seat around my money decisions. There was no way I was going to let nearly $70,000 of my hard-earned money slip through my hands over the next five years just because I liked eating out.

More than an hour later, I placed the blue bottle in the recycling bin. The word "Relax" seemed to jump off the label at me. Even this had become a habit. Not one I was willing to negotiate today, but the evidence was there—as seemingly innocuous line items on the credit card statements I'd just tucked into my budget binder, and in the recycling bin I carried to the curb every Monday morning.

Here's the funny thing about habits: some are slow-forming, and some show up like a race horse pounding around the corner at the Kentucky Derby. Some habits are healthy, and some are not. But all of them will become ingrained in your daily routines, and continue operating in stealth mode under the surface of your consciousness until you actually choose to look at them.

So, how do we dig up our habits and change the ones that aren't working? We start with an inventory of the routine behaviors and patterns you engage in while on autopilot—the behaviors hidden in your bank and credit card statements.

So, write in your notebook, "Every morning, I ..." and then fill in the itinerary for your morning routine, line by line. Include everything from the moment you get out of bed to the moment you get to work. Next, make a separate list of your routine throughout your workday, and another for your evening routines. Then, print out your bank and credit card statements for the last few months, and follow the trail of evidence.

WHERE HABITS REALLY COME FROM

Getting people to look at areas in their routines where they are being less than mindful is a big part of what I teach in this Pillar. We are always looking through that lens of finance, considering short- and long-term goals and how we can leverage our money to move in a positive direction, but what we uncover in this work is usually much deeper than dollars and cents.

When I worked with Jenny on her Habits pillar, we found that she had a habit of saying "yes" without hesitation whenever her boys, ages fourteen and fifteen, asked for the latest and greatest tech gadgets. They already had the newest gaming systems that had hit the market over the holidays—two at her house alone! They had brand-new iPhones that cost more than the laptop she and I were working on. Their latest "ask" was for new tablets—and Jenny was starting to cave.

She knew, after reviewing the Financial Pillar design we had created together, that she couldn't afford another "yes." She had to put her foot down, especially if she wanted to keep saving for the big tax bill she knew was going to hit on April 15. She hadn't paid her estimated taxes for the prior two quarters, in part because she was overspending on her boys. When I showed her that it wasn't impossible for her to come up with the money she needed, as long as she reined in her spending, her response was, "Hey, life is expensive, you know?"

Well, the tablets her kids wanted were expensive. But it wasn't Christmas. It wasn't either boy's birthday. They weren't graduating or hitting some other major milestone. So why did they need the tablets now?

When she asked them, their answer was, "All the other kids have them, Mom!"

As we talked more about this, it became clear to Jenny that, not only was her habit of saying "yes" affecting her bottom line, it was also creating a habitual mindset for her boys around immediate gratification. They wanted what they wanted, when they wanted it—and when they couldn't have it, it was painful for them.

During one session, she broke down in tears. "What I really want," she told me, "is to see them happy. I feel so horrible for ripping our family apart. I want them to be excited about spending time with me. If I can make them feel good, shouldn't I do it?"

This hadn't always been the case. Prior to the divorce, Jenny had worked pretty well with her husband at teaching the kids to save their own money for the things they wanted. But her desire to see them happy had led to this unhealthy habit of giving them things they wanted, even when she couldn't afford it. Her ex-husband had already pointed this out a couple of times after the boys rushed through his door with their new items in hand, but she didn't listen. She cared more about the *reward* this habit generated, which was to not see her boys sad or hurt.

Most habits are formed out of a need, desire, or craving for something. The habit is actually the action that rewards that craving, repeated over and over until it becomes part of a subconscious feedback loop. For example, when I looked at my bank statements, I noticed that I had a habit of going out to dinner on the nights when I didn't have my kids. I would call a friend to join me, and usually I would treat (because dinner was my idea). My desire, then, wasn't to have a meal. It was for companionship.

But there was even more to it. As I did more research into the nature of habits and how they're formed, I realized that companionship was actually the "reward" I was giving myself to sate my desire. My *actual* desire was not to be lonely.

The days when I didn't have my kids were my "trigger" days. In order to not be lonely, I created a new habit that ensured I could avoid that feeling.

Ugh. That one hit me like a ton of bricks.

While this habit was forming, I wasn't conscious of it as a habit; it simply evolved in response to my desire to not feel lonely. What started off as a good idea on one specific evening when I needed extra support had become a twice-weekly habit that was siphoning away my prosperity.

As I worked my way through more of the habits that were impacting my financial pillar, I realized that quite a few of them stemmed from a desire *not* to feel something. I was literally using my habits to numb myself to the pain and desolation I was feeling inside. And, because I was avoiding these feelings, they weren't getting processed. They were just sitting there, like dirty clothes at the bottom of a closet, getting ickier with each passing day.

Jenny's "yes mode" was based in avoidance, too—and reversing that habit brought up a lot of fears she'd been hiding. "What if I say no and they don't want to come to my house? What if they use it as a way to punish me? I'm not strong enough to handle that!"

I totally got it. I'd fallen prey to "yes mode" with my own kids at first; I had to learn how to say no, and they needed to learn how to hear it. So we talked about how many teachable moments Jenny was missing with her kids in these areas of money and life transitions. She had an opportunity to use this as a discussion starter around habits, finances, and what her boys' trying to keep up with the neighborhood kids was really about. They were also at an age where she could share with them her plan for creating a better financial reality for herself, and for them.

That initial "No" was hard—but after that, making positive changes was surprisingly easy. Today, Jenny is caught up on her tax bills, working her way out of debt, and giving her boys a new perspective on what "prosperity" really means.

Even Good Habits Can Become Bad Habits

My client Denise was one of those women I envied. She went to the gym every day, and looked like a fitness model. But when she got divorced, her once-healthy habit turned into an unhealthy obsession.

On the days when she didn't have her kids, Denise was at the gym twice a day, sometimes for hours at a stretch. She also started imposing stricter controls on what she was eating. We discussed this in one session when I noticed that, in a matter of only a few weeks, she'd dropped well below a healthy weight for her 5'7" frame.

"I want to do something positive, so I go to the gym," she said.

Since it was a "healthy" habit, going to the gym was the first thing that came to mind when she desired to fill her time. The gym was also a great place to meet new people and socialize. But instead of boosting her well-being, her habit was depleting her. As we explored how her healthy habit was turning into something less positive—a loss of nearly fifteen pounds from her already small frame, and the resulting need to budget for new clothes because everything she owned was suddenly too big—we talked about some different options she might explore.

We talked about how her fear of being "un-dateable" after her divorce led her to try to perfect her body. We talked about how she felt it was better to spend her free hours working out at the gym than at home alone. We talked about how feeling "in control" was important to her. And then, I invited her to think of some healthier ways to get the reward she was really seeking, which was to feel valued. At our next monthly session, Denise shared that she had taken a friend up on an offer to take a yoga class. She realized quickly that yoga offered her a place to not only work on her exterior strength, but also hone her inner strength. Because she had never tried yoga before, she had to accept herself exactly where she was. She signed up for a one month trial membership and found that she loved the variety of offerings. She also felt instantly connected to this new community. After a month or so, she was once again back to a healthy weight, and loving the time she was sharing with new friends at the studio. A year later, she made the decision to become a certified yoga instructor and take her love of fitness to a new level. While in training at the Kripalu center, she also met her new partner, who she's been dating for seven months!

My client Marge took a different healthy habit—a strong work ethic—and turned it into an escape portal. She'd just lost her Prince Charming to an old flame he'd connected with on Facebook. Riding on huge waves of grief, wondering how she'd failed to save the marriage she'd thought was as strong as Fort Knox, she dove into the one thing she knew she was great at: her job.

Six months after the divorce, she was working most nights until 1:00 a.m. She wasn't required by her employer to work more. She hadn't added a new territory or new accounts. She just worked because it gave her something productive to do. She certainly wasn't going to start dating; she wasn't ready for that. She wasn't going to zombify in front of the television, either. So she did what felt the most secure: she worked. And worked. And worked some more.

In our discussions around her Habits pillar, Marge was clear with me that she had no time for habits. She was all work and no play. She couldn't see that her work itself had become a habit—and an unhealthy pattern of avoidance. Her added hours at the office left no time for the therapy or coaching which could help her process and come to terms with the loss of her marriage. She was making herself so busy that she physically *couldn't* dig deeper and feel the pain she was carrying inside.

In order to move into her vision of prosperity after divorce, Marge was going to have to do something that felt completely antithetical to her goals: step away from her work until she could create healthy habits around it again.

"Are you willing to do a full-on reset here?" I asked.

She wasn't, at first. But as the stress of constant work began to take its toll on her mind and body, Marge changed her mind.

We looked closely at her Financial Pillar and saw that she had ample funds to take a break without compromising her future security. And so she did something that she'd always wanted to do: she toured the Amalfi Coast for twenty-one days. When she came back, she was well rested, and ready to start a new healthy habit: meeting once a week with her therapist. She also decided that she wanted to tweak some of her spending and add travel into her LifeStyle Re-Design Planning budget. This break in her workaholic habit created a new desire to live more fully.

No matter what emotions we are feeling, they will usually trigger in us some cues. These cues direct our behavior, and form new habits. So if your daily, weekly, and monthly habits don't support your bigger picture for prosperity after divorce— if they break your budget, or suck up all the energy you have to give—look to your feelings. If you are lonely, address the lonely. If you are sad, work on the sad. If your trust has been shattered, work on that. This will not only help you feel better, it will give you the support you need to break the habits that are undermining your prosperity.

Marketing Feeds our Habits

The last book I purchased wasn't one that was recommended to me. I didn't hear about it on NPR, or see a segment about it on the news. I bought it because it popped up on my Amazon feed.

The ad piqued my interest enough to read the blurb. Then, I read the sample, and ... *Voila!* Before I could even stop to think about it, I was clicking "Buy Now."

How did this happen? Because Amazon knows my habits.

Don't get me wrong, I love shopping online. It adds a level of ease to my life that makes a huge difference. But I'm also aware that online retailers use algorithms to fill up my feed with ads that match my spending habits. That book was a perfect example.

There are many ways that retailers are feeding your habits. QVC and HSN figured out early on how to take the habit of "impulse buying" and create a multi-billion dollar business around it. Now, Amazon, Wal-Mart, Target, and even Facebook have figured out how to increase sales using targeted ads and "recommendations." When we see products that match our habits (and feed our desires), we are more likely to buy. It's simple, really, and very effective—for the companies making the sales.

If we want to create prosperity and stabilize our Financial Pillar, we have to be aware that not everything that pops up in our Amazon feed is some kind of divinely guided sign pointing us toward our greater life vision. Sometimes, that may actually be true—but sometimes, it's just those pesky algorithms figuring out that you are the type of person who buys self-help books, or black tee shirts, or kitchen gadgets, or whatever. We need to become simultaneously more and less aware of the marketing that's happening behind the scenes every time we open our browsers. More aware, because we need to know what's happening, and how it feeds into our emotional buying habits. And less aware, because we need to learn to tune it out in order to make healthier financial choices.

EFTs: The Monthly Drain

There's another type of habit I want you to look at, and that's your monthly automatic charges.

Many companies have encouraged us to put things on EFT (Electronic Funds Transfer) to "simplify our lives" and make sure we don't miss payments. While this is actually helpful in many cases, including in our budgeting, those EFTs add up fast.

Think about some of the EFTs you might have coming out of your accounts right now.

- iTunes
- iCloud
- Audible

- Pandora
- Spotify
- Other apps for your phone or tablet
- Dropbox
- Premium cable channels
- Gaming fees for the kids (like Xbox Live)
- Gym memberships
- Other group memberships
- Monthly subscriptions to newspapers, magazines, and other publications
- Direct sales orders

Do you really need both iTunes Music *and* Pandora, or can you choose one or the other? Do you actually read the newspaper online, or do you just pay for the subscription? Do you actually watch all of those premium channels, or could you find the shows you love from a free online source? Sometimes, we don't even realize how much money we're wasting for services we don't need and won't miss.

In my case, my gym membership was sucking $34.95 out of my checking account every month—but was I going to the gym? No. I was using my bike and bag at home. And yet, that monthly draft kept coming out. I told myself I would make time here or there to actually go and use the facility, and that it would cost me more to cancel and re-enroll than to just keep paying. Sound familiar?

So, while you've got those bank statements out to look at your emotionally-based spending habits, take a look at your EFTs as well. I've seen clients cut upwards of $200 per month just by weeding out unnecessary recurring charges.

HOW TO CHANGE A HABIT

We've covered a lot of ground about how habits happen, how they evolve, and how marketing and EFTs sneakily feed them. Now, let's talk about how to change a habit.

Sometimes, changing a habit is easy once you know it's there. Other times, it takes a bit more effort and determination. And sometimes, the best way to change a habit is to compromise.

When I work with clients around this, I create a worksheet that shows them exactly how much money they have been spending, and where. We get to see the cost of that daily Starbucks habit, of eating lunch out five days a week, and of taking the kids out for fast food on the weekends. We see the cost of a smoking habit, of getting nails done every other week (a treat that often becomes a habit), and of indulging in that glass (or two) of wine every night.

None of this is about judging yourself. Yes, some habits (like smoking and excessive drinking) are bad for your health, but you already know that; I don't need to lecture you or pile on the guilt. In this Pillar, we're just looking at costs, line by line, and seeing where we can make improvements.

For example, if your daily latte habit is costing you $5.45 at Starbucks, what about getting a flavored coffee at Dunkin' Donuts or McDonalds for around $1.50 instead? That will save you $1,440 a year, and all you have to do is pull into a different drive-thru. If you're eating lunch out five days a week, how about trying to pack lunch just twice? You can still eat out three times, but you'll save $30 (or more) every week.

The more you find workarounds for the habits that are costing you the most money, the more you will see that habits and necessities are not the same thing. And hey, maybe you'll start using that Keurig after all!

The Bottom Line

Our habits affect our prosperity because they either strengthen or sap our Financial Pillar and monetary resources. But they also matter because they so often keep us from looking at what's really happening in our minds, hearts, and lives. Again, this work is all about getting real—so if you identify a habit that makes you want to run and hide, or if you get angry (at me, yourself, or someone else) every time you look at your bank statements, you'll know you've stumbled onto something big.

If you find yourself unwilling or unable to process the emotional needs and triggers behind your habits on your own, please seek help from a professional therapist. The more supported you feel in dealing with your habits on all levels, the more likely you are to make empowered choices that will move you toward your vision of prosperity.

Next, we'll look at the Work Pillar, and uncover how your work ties into your prosperity in obvious—and not-so-obvious—ways.

Chapter Eight

CLOSING THE GAP

(The Work Pillar)

When I made the announcement to my kids that I was going to be making a major life change and selling my half of my business so I could simplify our lives and spend more time with them, I expected a more elated reaction.

The scene I envisioned included them jumping up and down, and trumpets ringing in the air as the angels wept with joy. I envisioned my son doing the same "happy dance" he did when he scored a goal on the field. I imagined the beaming smile on my daughter's face.

But no! Out of the mouth of my youngest babe came chirping, "But Memère will still be driving me to my ortho appointments and practices, right?"

"No, son," I replied. "I'll be able to do that now."

After a few moments of silence, he shook his head. "Even if you stop working, I want Memère to take me." Apparently, he wasn't willing to forego the special stops with my mom at the donut shop where all of her retired friends hung out. Clearly, all of the old ladies cooing over him had inflated his preteen ego.

"Okay," I grumbled. "We'll ask her." Of course, I knew my mom would do it. She wouldn't want to be deprived of this precious bonding time any more than my son did.

Through all of this, my daughter had lingered in the kitchen, silently preparing our dinner from her Rachael Ray cookbook. When I finally caved to my son, she snickered.

"What's so funny?" I asked.

"You? Not work? You're going to be hospitalized from the shock to your brain."

I was crushed. It must have shown on my face, because they immediately rushed forward with hugs and back pats—but it felt like the kind of support that they would have given the kid who tried hard but struck out at every game.

I can't blame them. I wouldn't have believed me either.

Over dinner, they teased out their visions of what life would look like if I actually followed through with this crazy plan. My son commented that maybe I should use my free time to take cooking classes, so his sister wouldn't be the only decent cook in the family. My daughter mentioned that I should take a yoga class, since I'd been talking about doing it forever.

Then, as we cleared the dishes, a plea spilled from both their mouths at once: "Please, Mom, don't be too much *mom!*"

What did that mean, "too much mom?" Hadn't they gotten the shitty end of the stick all these years by not having a mom who was like the other moms—present, involved, eager to help with flash card drills and math homework? Didn't they want to be my biggest priority?

But being low on my new priority list was not what they were afraid of. They were afraid I would go from over-nurturing my business to over-nurturing them. After so many years of relative autonomy, that would feel crushing. They didn't want me to be that involved. They didn't need it.

Clearly, I had raised awesome and independent children. And with their admonition not to be "too much mom," they gave me permission to take my time to develop the "mom skills" that had been off my radar for far too long.

WHAT WORK LOOKS LIKE
AFTER DIVORCE

No matter what your work situation looked like before divorce, chances are it has changed—along with so much else in your life.

From the outside, my worked looked pretty much the same after I moved out—but inside, it was different. There was more pressure, more at stake. Now, I didn't just have to provide for one household, but for two—and I was still making the same amount.

Other women are faced with the fact that they haven't been in the workforce for years, even decades. For example, my client Susan was married in her early twenties. She worked for a short while, but when she and her husband decided to start a family, she volunteered to stay home with the kids instead of pursuing her career. It seemed like a win-win at the time, and she loved being a full-time mom.

Ten years later, Susan found herself a single parent with bills she had never seen before and a two-paragraph resume that *might* land her a job at a couple bucks above minimum wage, if she was lucky. Food, clothing, shelter, and saving for her kids' education (not to mention her own retirement) were all brand new concerns for her. She was struggling to manage her new life, and feeling boxed in by her limited options for work. Meanwhile, her ex was left with fewer expenses and more free time because the kids were living with Susan.

Staying at home with the kids was the right choice for Susan. It just didn't serve her well in the divorce, where her contribution to the household—which had seemed fair and equitable at the time—didn't carry the same weight as her ex's dollars-and-cents income.

Sadly, Susan might have found herself in a similar situation even if she had continued work when her kids were young. Women, especially mothers, often choose jobs that fit in with their responsibilities at home—which means working part-time, or having a full-time job they can walk away from at five o'clock, and shying away from responsibilities or opportunities for advancement that come with more hours and greater stress. The consequence of passing on advancement opportunities is, of course, a lower salary and fewer opportunities. This is probably fine—even desirable—in a partnership, but when divorce happens, suddenly these women realize how far the jump is between where they are and the career that will support an entire household (or even continue the lifestyle they had before divorce).

This poses even more of a challenge for people who are over fifty and divorcing—a segment of the divorce arena that has been on the rise in recent years and now carries its own label, "gray divorce."

My client Carol came to me at the age of sixty-three, eight years post-divorce. She needed guidance on how to handle her finances when her alimony ran out in less than two years.

During their twenty-eight year marriage, her ex-husband

had multiple affairs. When she turned fifty-five, she finally decided that she'd had enough. Their nest had emptied; her job as CEO of the household had come to an abrupt halt. She had replaced her role as Team Parent with a few days of volunteer work at the local children's hospital, but that wasn't enough to distract her from her husband's long hours and indiscretions. After a long year and a half of divorce proceedings, Carol was awarded the marital home, 30 percent of his retirement funds, (she had none of her own), and ten years of spousal support.

Eight years later, she still hadn't moved herself back into the workforce full-time. In addition to her continued volunteer work, she was working part-time in a small boutique owned by a friend, but most weeks her bouts of "retail therapy" offset what little she brought home. She was in a relationship, but had not remarried for fear that she would lose the spousal support that was paying her bills. Her biggest fears of being destitute were now ringing in her mind daily.

Carol knew she had to look at the bigger picture sooner rather than later. She booked a VIP Money Day Spa package with me so she could immerse herself in the LifeStyle Re-Design Planning process and get answers quickly. We spent the day working through her questions and looking at her Financial Pillar and budget, but we also carved out some time to look at personal development, and what she would need to change if she wanted to get out of her state of paralysis and take control of her prosperity.

We talked a lot about "value" that day. Carol had always been in a support role: first to her husband, then to her kids. With no one else's goals to work toward, she had been floundering for eight years. She simply didn't know what her gifts and talents were, let alone how to apply them to create financial security for herself.

We talked about her goals: supporting her current lifestyle after the alimony ran out, feeling more independent, and feeling like she was making a difference. We also looked at the bottom line—the income she absolutely needed to make to sustain herself. It was clear from all her years of volunteer work that she wanted to impact the lives of children and other vulnerable people, and that she was a natural nurturer. Now, it was a question of applying her unique gifts and talents to jobs that could create the income she needed.

At the end of our time together, Carol had a budget, income goals, and a list of potential jobs to explore. A few weeks later, she landed a job as a receptionist and intake manager for a local charitable organization. The salary didn't quite replace her alimony, but as long as she kept her retail job on Saturdays (and didn't spend her whole paycheck at the boutique) it would be enough to keep all of her bills paid and allow her to save money for retirement.

When we followed up a month after our original session, Carol was brimming with excitement. She was working at a job that would allow her to be financially solvent once the alimony stopped—and for the next two years, she could bank her entire paycheck to cushion her retirement account. More, she was using her naturally nurturing disposition to create a warm atmosphere at her new workplace, and support people in need who came through the doors.

WORK AND WORTH

Women who have been out of the workforce for many years often deal with pervasive feelings of unworthiness and uncertainty about their contributions in the workplace. This also translates to questioning their value in general.

The standards to which we measure ourselves as women are still, unfortunately, largely tied to old and outdated cultural ideals. More, they're tied to what we achieve for the people around us—our spouse, our kids, our community. We're taught that the best thing we can do for everyone else is to put ourselves last.

When divorce happens, that "everyone else" we've been working for either shifts dramatically or disappears altogether. Suddenly, we're no longer living for our spouse, but for ourselves (and possibly for our kids). If we don't feel, deep down, that we are worthwhile—that we are worth the same level of care, effort, and dedication we show to everyone else—it can undermine all of our other work toward prosperity.

If you're in a challenging position like Susan or Carol, looking at bottom-line numbers can help you determine the minimum income you need to be shooting for. It removes the question of "What am I worth?" and replaces it with the much more approachable question, "What do I need to make?" This in turn sets the stage for determining how your skill set can translate to real dollars and cents.

For example, if you were a homemaker for many years and love little kids, why not look into a nanny or day care provider position? If you have a degree that's been on the shelf for a decade, maybe you can take some refresher courses to brush up your skills and increase your viability in the job market. Sometimes, depending on your budget and long-term goals, it might make sense to go back to school and reeducate yourself in an area that interests you.

If you're really struggling with the notion of your own worth and value, it's important to seek the emotional support—professional or otherwise—that you need to lift your self-worth and feel empowered again. Once you do the inner work, the outer circumstances will feel much more approachable.

CLOSING THE GAP

Most divorced women I talk to say, "If there were more hours in the day, I'd *absolutely* work more."

While this willingness to do what it takes is awesome, it's not always the healthiest choice when it comes to creating real prosperity after divorce. (As you know, I've got some firsthand experience with that!) This is even more true when it comes to taking on a second job, and *especially* true when it comes to taking on a second job when you have kids.

There is no shortage of talent, dedication, or creativity among women who struggle with work situations post-divorce. The issue isn't that they don't want to work, and work hard— it's that the gap between their job prospects and the income they need to make is too wide to jump. Often, there simply isn't enough time in the day to earn what they need to make ends meet. More, the cost of child care can negate the value of a second job.

When it comes to divorce settlements, it's next to impossible to account for the broad social pressures that shape women's career decisions. It's statistically clear that women continue to be the primary caregivers for their children both during and post-divorce. This means increased expenses and a decrease in economic quality of life.

It's super hard when there isn't enough. But it's not sustainable to put in an eight-hour day at one job, and then put in another four (or more) hours in a side hustle when you also have kids to take care of and a home to maintain.

If your full-time workload and kids' schedules (dance, sports, etc) do not leave time for another part-time income-generating gig outside the home, go back to your budget. Review everything that isn't a basic necessity like food, heat, and rent. If you can shave things out of your budget, you may not need to earn as much as you expected. Other money-saving tricks like couponing, meal planning, and carpooling can also help here. Improving your cash flow can go a long way toward lowering your stress level around work and preserve your energy.

But, if the budget can't be adjusted (or if you don't want to adjust it), you'll need to find a way to close the gap between what you're earning and what you need to bring in. Spend a couple of hours brainstorming ideas. Write down everything, no matter how wild. Then, pick a few of the best ideas to explore further.

Here's what some of my clients have done to boost their incomes and bottom lines:

Shianne, Deborah, and Jill all took on remote work that they could do in the evenings at home. With our global economy and the barriers removed by the Internet, it's possible to work 24/7 without ever leaving your house. Virtual assistant work, freelance writing and editing, music reviews, customer service, and medical billing are just a few examples of remote gigs.*

Other clients have taught English as a Second Language (ESL) via Skype from 9:00 to 11:00 p.m. while their kids were in bed. Still more have partnered with direct sales companies that allow them to build their businesses via an online strategy instead of doing the standard home parties or door-to-door selling.

---

* Indeed.com is a great resource for these kinds of jobs. Type "remote only" in the search field to find jobs you can do from home.

Airbnb and other home-sharing services are another creative way to generate extra income. I met Ann when Jody and I booked her Airbnb in Newburyport for a weekend. Over morning coffee on the gorgeous deck, she asked me that standard question, "What do you do?"

When I said I helped women find prosperity after divorce, she lit up. Turns out, she had been divorced for three years and was on that discovery journey herself. She had actually set up the Airbnb as a means of staying in her marital home. Just eleven months earlier, she had invested about $10,000 to create a separate entry to her guest quarters (which were absolutely lovely!) and make it a dual space that could also be used for building her part time Reiki practice. The space became a treatment room on weekday evenings and an Airbnb rental on the weekends and the nights when she didn't have clients. Extremely proud of her ingenuity, she shared that, in the last six months, the combination had closed a $12,000 gap in her budget and actually brought in excess income, which she hadn't anticipated. "And," she went on, "I love meeting new people, and now I don't even need to leave home to do it!"

Using your spare hours or weekends creatively can help supplement your budget and keep you feeling empowered and optimistic. If keeping your lifestyle intact is one of your top priorities, you will find a way. Start with your income goal, and work backwards from there to create a strategy to close the gap. As Marie Forleo says, "Nothing is un-figure-outable!"

The Bottom Line

Your work is a foundational pillar of your prosperity after divorce, but it goes deeper than your weekly paycheck. It's all about how you see yourself in the world, and what you're willing and able to do to sustain yourself as an independent trailblazer in your own life.

Next, we'll explore the Family Pillar, which is interwoven with the Work Pillar and your budget in surprisingly deep ways.

Chapter Nine

MISSION: POSSIBLE

(The Family Pillar)

For some strange reason, after the tears stopped flowing and the reality that I would be moving out set in, the first question my kids asked me was, "What about our Super Bowl party?"

I'd just signed the lease on my new house on Strawberry Street, paid a hefty deposit and first month's rent, and wrapped up what was possibly the most difficult conversation I'd ever had with my children. Our traditional Super Bowl bash was the *last* thing on my mind.

"Can you stay here until the Super Bowl, Mom?" my son asked. "This is a really important year."

I don't even like football, but this was Super Bowl XLVI, the year the Steelers (my ex's favorite team) were playing. I agreed on the spot because I thought that this was a good compromise, and would give them time to digest this massive change. I could use the added time to move my things into the new place, anyway.

My son made this last Super Bowl *such* a big deal. He made signs. He designed a flyer and sent out invitations. He pushed me to purchase Steelers napkins, plates, and cups, and was pushing us to muster as many people as we could for this last hurrah. We hadn't spoken about my leaving more than a few times since that initial conversation, and this party seemed to be his only focus.

I, on the other hand, felt like a total scammer. This was our last show of the "good life" as a family, and by Tuesday, half of the attendees would know that I had moved out.

The whole event was painful. I did my best to keep it together, but there were multiple times when I ran to the bathroom and just cried. I cried because I truly loved my home. I cried because I loved hosting events like this, filling our house with the aromas of good food and the laughter of family and friends, and we would never have a party like this one again. I cried because I knew that my son was trying to show me how much fun our family was, and praying in his little heart that when his dad picked him up at day care on Monday afternoon he wouldn't be coming home to a house without Mom.

As you can imagine, the transition didn't go smoothly. Post-Super Bowl, my son lashed out at me with hurtful words, telling me he didn't want to come to my new house (but coming anyway), and when our forty-eight hours were up, telling me he wouldn't come back next time unless I promised him I would move home.

"Can't this just be a cooling-off thing with Dad?" he would ask. Then, he'd promise that, if I swore to move home again in six months, he would lose his attitude and be okay with the separation. It broke my heart.

In the home I was renting, I had an open, unfinished basement perfect for my boy to skateboard, ride a scooter around, or even play wiffle ball. Now, I'm pretty sure that my son knew I was no good at wiffle ball, and that sports are not my thing, but every time he would come over we'd venture into the basement and break out the bats. I wanted to connect with him, but it was like stepping into a boxing ring.

At first, he would be sure to pitch the ball in such a way that I would miss the catch and have to go fetch it. Then, he'd wind up like a major-leaguer and strike my leg. "Don't you like to play anything?" he'd taunt me.

It was clear that he wasn't getting what he needed from me. And so I marched my butt down into that basement four times a week, and got the crap beat out of me by a wiffle ball. I needed to stop saying "I can't" to my kids every time they wanted some of my time, and start saying "Yes." Even when it wasn't my idea of fun.

The great thing about my new relationship with "yes" was that I started to shed some of the guilt I'd been carrying since my kids were little. I had never really figured out how to balance work and my family life, but I was starting to see a glimmer of hope for myself in this area. I'd lost so many precious moments with my babies already; I was always split between them and my business. Like, "Yes, I'll be at the science fair today, but then I've got to run to a Chamber of Commerce meeting and I won't be home until nine o'clock." My kids lived in that space for many years, and they probably hated every bit of it.

I wanted my kids to know what hard work looked like. I wanted them to benefit from my efforts. I wanted them to know that I loved them enough to sacrifice my time, energy, and sanity for their well-being. But in that space of performing, I wasn't present. Now, in the basement with wiffle balls whipping at my face, I had to be—and I wanted to be, for all of our sakes.

Yes to ball in the basement. Yes to snuggling on the couch and watching a movie. Yes to shopping at the mall. Yes to playing the latest Wii game. Yes to friends sleeping over. I wasn't "yessing" just to make them happy—I was "yessing" to make *me* happy, and to start changing myself in an area that desperately needed work.

WHAT BALANCE REALLY LOOKS LIKE

Ask me if I believe that true balance is possible for any working mother, and I'll tell you, "Hell, no." That perfect, equitable, Zen-infused balance is a dream that gets sold to us by Instagrammers and mommy lifestyle bloggers.

But you can find *a* balance, if you're willing to be creative.

The more quality time I spent with my kids—honoring them, listening to them, and just being with them—the more the guilt and shame I'd been carrying around lifted. When I was with them, I was *with* them. Was it balanced with work? No, not every day. But the moments I created were enough to shift things in a big way, for all of us.

Only having my kids four days a week—and having to be the sole parent on the scene for those four days—shifted my perspective around being a mom. Divorce is like that; it blanks out the old canvas, and invites us to create something new. Part of my vision for prosperity was that ever-elusive balance between work and family. If I wanted to create that, I couldn't just keep saying, "I'm so sorry, but I don't have time." I had to *make* time.

Creating this balance takes effort. It takes commitment. It can also feel directly counterproductive when you're suddenly the sole breadwinner for your household. How the heck are you supposed to find quality time with your kids when you have to work nine to five (or longer) every day?

You do it by creating teachable moments.

Your kids are not outside of your divorce situation. They are part of your family unit, and part of the prosperous life you are creating. And while we don't want to shove our burdens (financial or otherwise) onto our kids, we can and should invite them into the "inner circle" of our daily lives, even when that means being a little bit vulnerable or imperfect.

Deanna approached me during the break at one of my workshops. After a morning of exploration, and having completed our exercises, she knew that she was going to have to tell her kids that they were not going to be able to take the cruise vacation she had already placed a $500 deposit on. There just wasn't enough money to pull it off. She was committed to creating stability, and putting another $4,500 on her credit card (on top of the already-heavy debt burden she'd inherited after her divorce) just didn't make sense.

It was going to be a difficult conversation, for sure. The trip had been coordinated by her daughter's dance school, and her daughter was going to feel left out if she didn't get to go. On top of that, Deanna would have to explain to the other moms why she was backing out. Ouch. More, she was disappointed that she would be missing out on an entire week having fun with her kids.

The smart financial choice—the choice that supported her prosperity—required her to admit that she didn't have it all together financially right now. I could tell that her pride was taking a hit. And, I couldn't downplay the fact that breaking this news to her kids was going to suck.

We talked about how this difficult decision would help her

create immediate stability, instead of making her more financially insecure by maxing out her credit card. We also focused on how she could approach the discussion with an element of goal setting at the forefront, and encourage the kids to participate in saving for next year's trip. This wasn't about the fact that Mommy couldn't make the trip happen. It was about the fact that they had to plan for big expenses as a family unit.

I suggested that Deanna print out a coloring sheet with a cruise ship on it, and break it into ten sections. Each section would represent $500 that needed to be saved. Once that goal was met, the section would be colored in by the kids. She agreed to try this approach and see how it went.

About three months later, I received an e-mail from Deanna. Although her kids were initially devastated by the news and many tears were shed, in the end, they rallied, and started diving into money-saving and income-generating activities. They hung the coloring sheet on the fridge and were excited to see it filled in. They organized two yard sales over the summer, and her son offered a portion of his proceeds from mowing neighbors' lawns to make up the remaining money for that section and meet the $500 goal. Deanna wrote, "They have learned that goal setting and progress feels good. I know that they will apply this for the rest of their lives, starting with how to handle paying for college!"

More, Deanna got to spend a *ton* of quality time with her kids talking about and executing these financial activities. They may not have been on a cruise ship, but they were still bonding as a family. She was able to create a balance that didn't jeopardize her vision for prosperity, and which actually brought them closer together. It was a win-win!

The work we do here in the Family Pillar moves beyond money and into the deeper realms of family growth. I'm most moved by the overflow of lessons and knowledge that touch our lives in areas that define prosperity beyond what we could previously imagine. Deanna didn't just find a way to gloss over a difficult situation. She created an opportunity to learn alongside her children and watch them apply real life lessons as they saved for next year's trip. Instead of working overtime or picking up a second job to give her kids what they wanted, she created a new balance to give them what they needed—an opportunity to participate alongside her in creating their new family future.

WANTS VS. NEEDS FOR YOUR KIDS

As you've probably guessed by reading the stories so far in this chapter, creating balance in the Family Pillar isn't about giving your kids everything they want. It's about giving them what they need.

Discerning the difference between the two isn't always as easy as you think. As we discussed in the Emotional and Habits Pillars, saying "yes" to everything is not a good way to create balance, stability, or real prosperity. But neither is saying "no" all the time, especially when we do it without giving context.

Why? Because kids take everything to heart.

When my client Emeline, a CPA, divorced her husband, she went into total financial lockdown. She spent hours poring over the raw numbers, wondering how it was all going to work. The more scared she got, the tighter a lock she kept on her wallet. Gone were the days of movies, shopping trips, and family excursions. Buying a treat at the grocery store that wasn't on the shopping list was a no-no. Everything got scaled back to the least expensive version of itself, even the toothpaste and shampoo.

As you can imagine, this created a lot of tension in Emeline's household. Her teenagers took the budget cuts to heart. "They think I'm angry with them. They keep saying that I don't love them anymore, that I don't care about what they want," she told me. "But I'm just scared that there won't be enough. I have to make sure we're covered if something happens. They don't understand why they can't have the allowance they used to have, or go to the movies with their friends. But if I give them money this week, I'll have to do it every week, and ..." She shook her head.

Many of us default to controlling behavior when we get scared or uncertain. We try to plan for everything. Most of the time, this is a good thing—but when we're hanging on to money out of pure fear, and not enjoying our lives in big and small ways that still honor our budget, that's actually counterproductive to our prosperity. Why? Because we won't feel prosperous, and we'll still feel out of control.

When we looked at Emeline's finances under the microscope of the Financial Pillar and the LifeStyle Re-Design Planning budget, we found that she actually had far more money than she had disclosed at first. Turns out, she hadn't been counting her alimony payments in the budget she'd been keeping ("Because what if he stops paying?" she explained). She actually had several hundred dollars coming in per month that were simply sitting in an account, waiting for the other shoe to drop.

"What if you were to take some of that money and do something fun with your kids this weekend?" I asked her.

"They would be really excited," she admitted.

"You don't have to spend it all—but what if you took ten percent of that alimony money and made it a 'family fun fund?' And what if you explained to the kids why you're freezing up the budget right now? Maybe let them see what we've created today? Would that help them understand what's happening?"

Emeline admitted that it might. So she did something that she'd never done before: she talked to her kids about money, not in theoretical terms, but in real numbers. She admitted her fear around not having enough, and explained how those fears were affecting her actions around her kids' allowances and the household budget. Her kids immediately responded to being included in the conversation. They still didn't agree with the lockdown budget, but the tense conversations became a lot less frequent, because they knew that Emeline's actions weren't triggered by something they had done, or because her feelings toward them had shifted. Her fifteen-year-old daughter even started looking for a small part-time job so she could pay for outings with her friends and "not stress out my mom when I ask for money."

The Bottom Line

Your financial life doesn't just affect you; it affects your family, too, sometimes in unexpected ways. Maybe you need to work more, or (as in my case) work less. Maybe you need to save more, and spend less. Maybe you need to make some hard choices, like Deanna, or admit to the fears that are driving you, like Emeline. These changes are a natural part of the evolution of your life after divorce. And, if you make choices that are aligned with your LifeStyle Re-Design Planning and your goals for the future, you'll continue to evolve toward your biggest vision of prosperity.

Next, we'll look at the best and biggest support system you can utilize in your life, now and in the years to come …

Your spirituality.

Chapter Ten

FAITH IN YOUR FUTURE

The Spiritual Pillar

I have always considered myself a spiritual person, but I didn't have a true spiritual "practice" until fairly recently. I was raised Catholic by my mother—who, like her mother, was extremely devout—but I was always questioning the man-made laws of the Church. I stopped attending mass at eighteen, and while I wasn't necessarily "wounded by religion" (to use the term coined by my good friend, Pastologist Terrilyn Curry Avery), I was seeking a connection with my Divine Creator, not some old-man God who was ready to beat my behind with a stick if I stepped out of line, and who required a priest to speak to him on my behalf because I wasn't good enough to talk to him directly.

(Phew! Let me tell you how my eighteen-year-old self *really* felt.)

When I was twenty-five, my daughter was born. She was ten-and-a-half weeks premature, and at just three pounds two ounces, she was tinier and more fragile than I could ever have imagined a baby being. She spent thirty-four days in the NICU, which was more than an hour away from our home. I prayed and prayed that God would not take her from us. I begged, pleaded, and offered to take her place. I wondered, deep down, if this was my punishment for leaving the Church. But each time that thought arose, a knowing voice inside me reminded me that my God was a loving God; my only job was to show up for my daughter, and trust that everything would be okay.

When my little girl finally came home, we wanted to have all of the "normals"—like a baby shower (which happened after her release from the hospital, since I was still supposed to be pregnant) and a baptism. Six months later, I felt like a hypocrite for not going back to church regularly, but I still sensed that it wasn't the right place for me.

Six years later, my son was born. We decided not to do a baptism for him. My grandmother (God rest her soul) used to give me the side-eye when he was colicky, and mutter under her breath, "It's because he's not baptized." Eventually, she and my mom broke out the holy water and did the baptism them-selves in my mom's kitchen. (The colic, of course, continued.)

I didn't bring my kids to church regularly, but they didn't lack spirituality. We prayed together, and served in our community together. We opened our home on holidays to anyone who didn't have family to go to. We forgave those who wronged or upset us. We respected others; we loved.

Every evening, we snuggled into bed and read a book. Sometimes, it was a Dr. Seuss story. Sometimes, it was an entry from the children's Bible I'd purchased at a yard sale. Sometimes we read *A Course in Miracles*. Our bedtime prayers were for love, light, healing, peace, and protection.

As they got older, the kids incorporated a gratitude journal into our daily routine. It sat on our kitchen counter, and every day we would add a new entry, separately or together. At dinner, we always shared two things about our day, one positive and one challenging, and offered gratitude for both. We listened to Dr. Wayne Dyer's *There's a Spiritual Solution to Every Problem* so often on the way to and from school that whenever they heard Wayne's voice on the television they would come running, asking, "Is he going to tell Tommy's story tonight?" When my daughter hit her teens, I would frequently see psalms or affirmations written in black and pink Sharpie across her large bathroom mirror. My mother's heart swelled. She also found a church youth group through her best friend that felt like a home space for her, and attended there for about three years. I was happy that her foundation was strong enough for her to discern a spiritual path that worked for her, even if the rest of the family wasn't walking the same path.

Post-divorce, we continued our daily practices in my new house. We purchased a new, leather-bound journal to record our gratitudes, hung a new "House Rules" sign, and started an "evidence journal" where we recorded things that we knew were Divine signs. Cheryl Richardson's Grace Cards became a staple in our living room, and we even shared them with our friends. They looked forward to pulling two random cards out of the deck and sharing aloud the beautiful reminders of Grace that were specific to them that day.

Then, my daughter's migraines started.

As I shared in Chapter Three, these left her in horrible pain, unable to go to school or enjoy the normal parts of her teenage life. After she'd been battling them for more than a year, I started talking to God about them in my daily meditation/

prayer sessions. I begged for intervention and guidance. I was feeling emotionally broken, ridden with guilt over having to leave my daughter bedridden in our new home while I went off to work each day. I wondered if she was being punished for my decision to divorce (which is against the law of the Church).

"Why her?" I asked. "Why not me?"

Just as it had when my daughter was a tiny preemie fighting for life in the NICU, a deep knowing came over me. I was not being punished. My God was a loving God, and He was right here with me in this storm.

I moved from my cross-legged position to lay down full-length on the deck. Tears streamed down my cheeks as I lay there, broken, in silence. Maybe I wasn't being punished, but I still had no answers ... and I needed them.

And then, I heard a quiet, loving whisper that was nonetheless loud and clear in my mind: *"Let your daughter come to you the way you are coming to me. I do not push myself on you, yet you push yourself on her. When she comes to you, ask her what she needs, and what she wants to do. She already knows. You're just not available in the way she needs. You're so busy trying to figure it all out that there is no room for listening."*

Bam! I knew in that moment that God had spoken to me, clearly and directly. Usually I saw signs of Divine presence through other people and circumstances in my life, but I now knew that such was the norm because I never slowed down for long enough to *listen*. My meditation and prayer times were carved into my crazy day, and while they were better than nothing, those 14.8 minutes didn't give God much room to speak. Today, though, He hit the proverbial nail on the head.

I had been pushing my daughter to fight the migraines with mind over matter. I had been pushing her to push through. I had been taking her phone away, because if she was in too much pain to go to school, she was definitely too sick to be texting and posting on Facebook. With every push, I was pushing her away. She needed *me*, not more solutions. She understood her own pain. She was a frequent patient at the local emergency room because the migraines caused hours of vomiting that dehydrated her to the point of needing an IV. I, on the other hand, had probably only had a handful of headaches in my life, all of which were the result of too much vodka the night before. How could I claim to know best here?

Two days after my surrender, my daughter opened a conversation with me while we were sitting on the couch watching our weekly episode of *Gilmore Girls*. She had been invited to spend the evening at a girlfriend's house, but didn't think she was going to go.

"Why not?" I asked.

"Mom, do you know what it's like to be fifteen and walk into your friend's house with a Ziploc bag full of medicine? Not a makeup bag—a medicine bag!"

I wanted to reply, to tell her that her friends understood— but instead, I listened.

She shared that she felt so alone. She'd missed over a hundred days of school at this point. Prayers and positive affirmations weren't helping. The doctors, who'd put her on three new meds and started giving her injections in her legs, weren't helping. Therapy wasn't helping. *I* wasn't helping.

"What do you think we should do?" I asked her.

She answered in a rush, like she'd always had the answer but had been holding it inside. "Get me off all of these meds. They are *not* working. Get me to a naturopathic doctor, and get me back to my church. I need prayers and healing!"

I couldn't believe my ears. My fifteen-year-old was so strong, and so clear about her own inner knowing, that there was no more question about what needed to be done. I hugged her and promised that I would take her lead, and that we would start with church the next day and the naturopath on Monday.

I went with my daughter to church on Sunday, and I understood why she liked this place of worship. I felt like my soul had been awakened by her faith, and now I received the message of faith in a new way. After the service, my daughter walked up the aisle to where the pastor was standing, and asked for prayers. They motioned me forward and asked me to lay my hands on her alongside theirs. We prayed for her full restoration, so she could fully be who God meant her to be in this life. And I knew those prayers were heard, and that they would be answered. It was an incredibly powerful moment to witness, and it left me both in awe of my own child and fully committed to tapping into my own inner wisdom in a much bigger way.

BECOMING YOUR PROSPERITY

What the heck does the story I just shared have to do with prosperity after divorce?

Everything!

It is in the midst of our deepest sorrow, and our wildest storms, that we have an opportunity to tap into our own knowing—to surrender all our pushing, and open to a better way of being, doing, and learning. When it comes time to build our vision of prosperity—whatever that looks like—we need to be connected to our own inner wisdom, and to some form of higher power (God, Goddess, Source, The Universe, etc.). If we aren't, we will just go on living as we have always lived, and creating the same experiences we've always created, because our compass won't be set to our own "true north."

I've said all along that prosperity isn't just about money. It's about defining and honing all six Pillars of Prosperity so that you can have a deeper, richer, more meaningful life. This Pillar—the Pillar of Spirituality and your inner world—is where all of the external work we've done in the other five Pillars gets rooted and becomes real.

If you don't change the way you think and feel to match your vision of true prosperity, your actions—no matter how on-track they are—won't stick. You won't be able to sustain them. And so, inside your own mind and heart, you need to start to *become* the person who lives in your prosperous future, and then take action from that place. Only then will you be able to truly see and feel the value of the work we've done in all the other Pillars, and sustain the new habits, mindset, and actions we've created together.

This isn't an instantaneous process. You are constantly evolving, and you always will be. But you have to start somewhere, and there's no better time than now.

We all have an inner guidance system and an inborn ability to tap into the Divine. Not all of us use it. We push aside this connection because of our bad experiences with religion (which is different from spirituality, by the way; religion is collective and man-made, while spirituality is individual), or because we've learned through abuse, trauma, or social conditioning not to trust ourselves. However, our internal guidance system hasn't disappeared just because we've forgotten or ignored it, or because the "spiritual" parts of ourselves have been on sabbatical. We just need a little TLC and regular practice to get that connection plugged in and running again.

How do you know that you're on the right track? You start with the small things, like validating the intuition that led you to this book. When you read the title, "Prosperity After

Divorce," some part of you knew that this book could help you chart your path to a new, exciting, prosperous life—and now you're actually doing it!

Now, think of all the other times, places, and encounters in your life recently that have been "right" for some reason. There are no coincidences. You probably recognized, at some level, the feeling of "rightness" when you bumped into an old friend after a hard day, or when that check arrived just in time to keep you from overdrawing your account. Remember the inner "tingle" you got when these things happened? That's your inner guidance system at work.

To get more active with this inner listening, especially if you're out of practice, use this morning prayer from *A Course in Miracles*. I started using this after my surrender moment, and it has allowed me to reach that state of knowing and feeling God's presence daily. Things got so much easier when the burden to make things happen no longer felt like it was all on me!

Morning Prayer

Each morning, sit quietly, close your eyes, and ask:

- Where would you have me go today?

- What would you have me do?

- What would you have me say, and to whom?

Then, say something like "Thank you God for reorganizing my thoughts and guiding me." Then, take a deep breath, and release all of the tension in your body.

The more you work with this simple exercise, the more connected to your Higher Power and your inner knowing you will feel.

Divorce Sucks, But …

Divorce does not define the rest of our lives.

Who we are, and what we do with our time on earth, is what defines us.

Let that sink in. Grasp it. Make it your mantra. Find your power in it.

When times were really rough for me, I found a lot of solace in positive quotes and affirmations. One of my favorites was from Jeremiah 29:11: "'*For I know the plans I have for you,' declares the Lord: 'Plans to prosper you and not to harm you, plans to give you hope and a future.'*"

Whatever positive messages resonate with you, place them around you—in your home, in your car, in your wallet, at your desk. Let them remind you that you can co-create, with your own Higher Power, the life you want, and that all things are possible.

YOU ARE A CO-CREATOR, NOT A DEPENDENT

Regardless of who you are or what job you currently do, you have the ability to create your vision of prosperity after divorce. Whether you are a professional in a career with fluctuating income, a stay-at-home mom trying to meld a return to the workforce with your core values around raising your children, or a "gray divorce" survivor negotiating a new lease on life, you *can* do this work, and you *can* create your prosperity.

Whether you are in the middle of your divorce, or your divorce is ten years in the past, you can make your prosperity real *now*. Your journey begins with creating financial stability and consistency—the work we've done in the last five Pillars. This is my expertise; it's what I teach, and I know it works.

But, here's the catch: in the time I've spent with hundreds of women (and men) creating their prosperity plans, I've learned that *belief,* not budget, is the biggest factor in creating prosperity and success. You can't even start walking the path toward prosperity until you decide, deep within yourself that:

- You can do this.

- You are worthy of this.

- You have the power to create the life you want.

- The only thing keeping you from creating prosperity starting *right now* is the belief that you can't do it.

Leading others in this Pillar of LifeStyle Re-Design Planning is not something I ever thought I would do. It was only after I learned to truly listen to my God and my inner guidance that I was able to create real prosperity after my divorce. I had money, but I was burned out, exhausted, forty pounds overweight, and failing my kids. After my moment of surrender on the porch, and my daughter's brave step toward healing in her own empowered way, everything inside me shifted. Gradually, I became able to tune into not only the strongest messages from my Higher Power, but my own deepest desires around my life, my time, and my prosperity.

It was this deep inner connection that revealed how much I wanted to be present for my kids, my partner, and myself. It was this knowing that led me to sell my business and start down this path of teaching and guiding others to find their own prosperity. In taking this leap of faith, I believe that I have found what I am truly called to do.

Was it scary? Of course! Are there times when my inner critic shows up and screams at me from her podium? Sure. I hear from her all the time. She says things like, "What could you possibly have to offer?" and "Really? Why you?" She and her mean-girl friends will have a field day in my brain if I let them—but I don't. I remind them that I'm in charge here, and that I've got a Higher Power on my team who can out-class them any day.

This feeling of being in charge is actually one of the scariest parts for many of the women I work with in my LifeStyle Re-Design Planning process. They have a deeply-ingrained belief that they are not enough—that they don't have enough, can't do enough, and can't be enough. And so, when it comes time to step up and design their new life, they balk.

It's not surprising to me that these feelings of inadequacy surface when our vows of forever are broken, and when we have to look at the black and white (or red) picture of our lives as they now are. It feels like enough to stop us from breathing some days. But this part of the LifeStyle Re-Design Process is actually my favorite. Why? Because I love helping women move from a state of fear and confusion and into to a state of decision, control, and empowerment—and reminding them that their faith and divine connection is their best resource for making this shift, regaining their financial footing, and creating prosperity.

Now, here's the reality check: your Higher Power is a *resource*. S/He is not a maid who cleans up your messes, and not the General Manager of your life. It might sound harsh, but you can't pay the bills on faith alone. Prayer won't magically change the numbers in your budget columns, especially if you refuse to change your habits. Sometimes, miraculous help *does* show up—but if that's your only plan for creating prosperity, you're in trouble.

The Blessings of Action

In my walk with divorced and divorcing women, I see a lot of this "sit and wait" approach. Sometimes it's because of fear paralysis; sometimes it's because of faith; sometimes it's because of upbringing or experience. But waiting for God to step in is never a sustainable answer to their problems.

When I met Maria, she was stuck in this waiting game. As a gift to her, a dear friend who had taken one of my classes paid for her session with me. She shared, "Maria is incredibly talented and giving. I feel she is capable of so much more. But she is a faithful woman, and I think that's keeping her stuck."

How could faith be keeping someone stuck? I wondered.

I soon had my answer.

Maria had been divorced for eleven years, and her children were grown. Her alimony had run out a year earlier. She was two months behind on her rent, was unable to heat her apartment, and would soon be facing eviction if something didn't change. She had been relying heavily on family and friends to help her financially for years, but that reservoir was drying up.

She had zero savings. Zero freedom. Zero joy.

But huge amounts of faith.

In our initial phone conversation, Maria made it clear that she believed God would continue to provide all that she needed, and that she would be just fine. She only agreed to meet with me because she didn't want to seem ungrateful for her friend's gift.

It was obvious that she didn't want to budge from her position. It was also obvious (to me, at least) that the numbers weren't working. If she didn't find a way to increase her income, she was going to be out on the street.

In our time together, I asked about her gifts and talents, looking for a way I might help her expand her thinking. She shared that she had been the children's youth minister at her church for fifteen years, and told stories of how she was able, through creativity, to bring the children to a place of exploring their own gifts and talents. She opened her Facebook page and showed me photos of her incredible artwork and photography. I found myself drooling as I scrolled through pictures of the farm-to-table dishes she clearly loved to create.

I was in the presence of a powerhouse artisan who made Martha Stewart look like Kermit the Frog. But she wasn't wowing the world with her vibrant creations. She was working in a school cafeteria twenty hours a week for minimum wage and no benefits. She didn't get paid during the entire summer break; instead, she collected unemployment benefits, which were even slimmer than her normal paychecks.

"Have you considered finding another job to get you through the summers?" I asked.

"No one will hire me for twelve weeks," she replied.

"What about looking for another part-time job to supplement your income year-round?"

"I'm fifty-four years old with no college degree. I had to drop out of school to raise my three kids. That was the path God chose for me. It's been hard, but I'm stronger for it."

I couldn't believe what I was hearing. Here was a woman with gifts and talents most people would kill for, but she wasn't using them because she'd decided that her path was one of suffering. Actually, it made me a little bit mad—not at her, but at the belief system that made it easier for her to surrender into that suffering than to shine like the bright light she was.

I suggested to Maria that she could start exploring these amazing talents and use them to help her find more income. She loved working with children, so nanny or *au pair* work was a definite possibility. So were summertime catering gigs;

in New England, plenty of seasonal businesses take on short-term employees. The big positive was that, since her kids were already out of the house, she only had her own schedule and needs to worry about; she didn't need to be home to pick anyone up from school or sports, or cook dinner for the family.

By the latter half of our call, she was willing to dip her toes into the scary work of charting her immediate financial needs, as well as peeking at a bird's-eye view of her overall situation and the security she'd like to create in the near future. She even threw in a few "wants." Working backwards from the "magic number" that would pay her rent and expenses and allow her to create a retirement nest egg, we explored some possible employment options and figured out how much she would need to make in order to meet her goals (and actually have some fun, too).

Over the next few weeks, Maria made a radical transformation. She applied for more than twenty-five full-time and part-time jobs, and was soon offered a job as the activities director at a local nursing home. This provided her with an extra thirteen hours per week of work, for a monthly gain of $780 and an annual gain of $9,360. It also provided healthcare benefits and paid time off for holidays and personal time after the first ninety days.

She also interviewed with a local caterer to explore her passion for cooking. In their discussion, the owners shared their vision for expanding their business to include cooking classes in the community. Maria mentioned her prior work with leading and teaching children and how this was also one of her dreams—and guess what? The caterers hired her to teach two cooking classes on Saturday mornings to children in two different age groups. She was the gift they were waiting for to make their new vision come to life! This side gig also brought in another $5,000 a year for Maria, while opening the door for her to combine her love of cooking with her skills in teaching.

When I caught up with her a few months later, Maria was a very different woman. Motivated, excited, and bursting with energy, her smile lit up the whole room—but one thing hadn't changed. Her faith was just as rock-solid as it had been all along.

"I know God sent you to me," she said.

"I think so, too," I replied, "But only to show you what you were capable of all along."

"The Lord helps those that help themselves," she reminded me with a smile.

I couldn't have agreed more.

***

Here's the thing about faith: it will carry you through anything. But it won't *make* things happen, and it won't magically change your reality. In order to get God/the Universe/ your Higher Self working on your behalf, *you* need to take those first, uncertain steps.

And that's really what faith is all about, isn't it? The not-knowing? Walking through uncertainty with conviction, and trusting that it will all be okay in the end?

If this is speaking to you, I encourage you to step out of the waiting and start exploring. Have faith that *you*, like Maria, have divinely-appointed gifts and talents that you can leverage to create your unique vision of prosperity—gifts that can bring in an income to help create the financial stability and security you need and desire. I truly believe that when we know the value of our gifts, it is easier to step into receiving what is available to us.

DISCOVER (AND MONETIZE)
YOUR UNIQUENESS

There is only one of me, and only one of you.

I love knowing that each of us is a unique piece of the Divine fabric that is life. We get woven into a tapestry, with each one of us touching others' threads in various inspiring ways. When we are all using our innate gifts and talents, we work together to create a beautiful picture that becomes our reality.

But here's the thing: do you really believe that you have something to offer?

If you haven't had people in your life who are willing and able to speak positively about you, or if you're carrying old beliefs inherited from family or faith about whether you are "good enough" to deserve prosperity and happiness, listen up:

You are valuable.

You are worthy.

You are loved.

And you *can* create the life you desire simply by doing what you are already great at. *"For God has not given us a spirit of fear and timidity, but of power, love, and self-discipline."* (2 Timothy 1:7)

As you start to put all of the Pillars of LifeStyle Re-Design Planning into play, it is imperative that you look deeply and clearly at your spiritual mindset around money, worth, and worthiness.

As spiritual beings we are meant to grow and prosper here on Planet Earth. We are meant to share our gifts with others. We are meant to live fully.

Having money and prosperity is not evil. Maybe you were raised to think it is—but those beliefs that money and rich people are "bad" are simply moldy leftovers from a church and feudal culture that no longer exists. Those beliefs were so pervasive that they were carried across oceans and through hundreds of years—until your parents, church elders, and others shared them with you.

Maybe you had to listen to gossip about how "hoity-toity" the neighbors were after your parents saw their new Oldsmobile in the driveway. Maybe you listened to sermons about how it's easier for a camel to fit through the eye of a needle than for a rich man to enter Heaven. But this is a falsehood that feeds into all the other judgments you're making about yourself and others. These punishing beliefs flow over, not just into your Financial Pillar, but into other areas of your life such as habits, emotions, and even new relationships.

The world needs women who are strong earners. Collectively, we can be an answer to many of the problems we see in the world today. But although taking the reins of our own power is a great thing, we can't do it in the old, masculine way—and why would we want to, anyway? What we are working with is *not* what we want our children to inherit, so we need to do things our own way.

So take a long, hard look at who you are, and what you bring to the table. Shush those voices that tell you you're not enough, or that owning your value is prideful (and therefore a sin). And once you have a handle on what makes you different than anyone else, start asking yourself and whatever Higher Power you're connecting with, "How can I use these gifts to make a difference, make a living, and find my vision for prosperity?" If you surrender into the silence, and listen—*really* listen beyond the chatter of your own thoughts—I promise, the answers will find you, just like they found me.

DAILY PRACTICES

To help you tune in to your gifts and quiet your mind enough to receive your inner knowing and the voice of your Higher Power, I've included some very simple meditation and prayer exercises in the last part of this chapter. Try them, and adapt them to suit your own faith, rituals, and preferences. It's less important *how* you meditate, and more important that you just do it, because sitting in the stillness is the gateway to everything you need to know about your prosperous, amazing future.

Prayer Journaling

For many years, "prayer time" for me was simply closing my eyes for two minutes, taking a few deep breaths, and then writing in my journal for about ten minutes. It was a daily communication with my Divine Creator where I was able to pour out all my fears, frustrations, and challenges, and share all my hopes and dreams. Once everything was out of my head and onto the page, I would sit quietly for a few more minutes to let any messages come through. As I got better at listening, I was given amazing guidance nearly every day.

Over time, my prayer entries evolved from longing for strength and guidance to statements of hopefulness and joy. I loved that I could pull my past journals from the shelf and see the evidence of my progress.

If this practice calls to you, get a new journal to dedicate to this practice. If you're not sure where to start, you can work with one or more of the following prompts:

- Growing up, what were some of the things you remember your parents saying about money?

- Were you raised to think that having wealth or affluence was a bad thing or a good thing?
- Do you have a belief that money is not spiritual?
- Do you believe that God wants us to struggle?
- What is your greatest fear about creating wealth?
- How much money is "too much" in your mind?
- How would you like to change your family legacy around money mindset?

Commit to writing for at least five minutes every morning. Then, once your words are on the page, listen to your inner knowing and write down any additional thoughts or messages that appear. You may be surprised at how connected you already are!

Simple Beginner's Meditation

While difficult for some of us, mediation is an invitation to allow ourselves quiet time. It allows us a "healing gap" where we can surrender our chaos for a few minutes and exchange it for an open space. We can close our eyes, take a breath and name that space as sacred. In this space we can invite in our God, guides, and angels for wisdom, clarity, and support, and honor ourselves by exploring the depths of our inner knowing.

Meditation is different than prayer. Prayer is active; it involves you speaking or asking. Meditation is the quiet space of receiving—from yourself and from God.

If you have trouble just being quiet (as I did for a long time), seek out guided meditations. There are literally thousands on YouTube, and thousands more on apps you can easily download for free onto your phone or tablet. You can choose meditations for positivity, clarity, deep sleep, money attraction, you name it. Just find something that resonates with you and drop into a space where you can completely pay attention—no multitasking! Meditation time is your time to get connected and centered, and receive information about your growth and prosperity.

If you want to try a simple visualization on your own, here is a meditation to meet your Future Self and ask her about your road to prosperity.

> Find a comfortable position, either sitting upright or laying down. Close your eyes and take a few clearing breaths in and out. Count to five on each inhale, and again on each exhale.
>
> Imagine a white or golden light of relaxation flowing through your body. It enters through the crown of your head and seeps into your throat, to your neck, down to your arms and into your fingers. Through your chest, back, buttocks, and down your legs and feet. The light fills you, and you feel fully relaxed.
>
> When you are relaxed, visualize your favorite place. Maybe you are walking a path to the beach, or standing in an open field of wheat, with the stalks swaying in the warm summer breeze. Stand there, and invite your future self to come and join you. This Future Self is from the most positive and powerful possible future accessible to you.
>
> Your Future Self accepts the invitation. She is standing in front of you. Greet her, and let her know you have some things to ask her.
>
> You can ask questions like:
> - What does life look like where she is?
> - How does she spend her days? Her evenings and weekends?
> - What does she do for work? Fun? Creative projects?

- Is there anything she can tell you about how to use your biggest gifts and talents?
- Where do you need to pay closer attention?
- What do you need to let go of?
- Is there any other advice or guidance she wishes to give?

This exercise is designed to get you more deeply connected with your intuition and internal knowing. In order to create our prosperity after divorce, we must come into a space of *allowing*. We must create a space to grow. We must align with the prosperous future we want in our hearts and minds, so that the actions we take in our lives actually bear fruit, and don't fall away like the latest fad diet.

The Bottom Line

Money and spirituality are inseparable, because our spiritual practices connect us to the deepest parts of ourselves. If we are disconnected, fearful of Divine judgment, or stuck in that disempowered "waiting place," none of the work we have done in the other five Pillars will stick.

So, go back through the exercises in all of these Pillars, applying a spiritual lens. What do you believe about your financial situation, and how is that impacting your prosperity? Where can you make room for Divine guidance to come through? Where do you need more faith, and where do you need more action?

Have faith in yourself and in the gifts you were given. Be willing to see clearly, and be open to learning new ways of being, doing, and creating. Your prosperity, like everything in your life, is in your hands.

Are you ready to make the magic happen?

Part III

THE GRAND
RE-DESIGN

Chapter Eleven
YOUR PROSPERITY QUOTIENT

———◆◈◆———

A few months ago, driving back from a workshop I was teaching, I parked the car at the foot of my winding 900-foot driveway and sat there, gazing up at my home. Surrounded by meadows and woodland, it's a true country house with five bedrooms, a wraparound porch, and lots of privacy—perfect for me and my blended family. I'd been living there since 2010, but that day it seemed brand new to me. I remembered moving in on Valentine's Day, pausing in this very spot to gaze up at my amazing new house, and reflecting on all I had been through to get here.

If you had told me back then that my prosperity would look like a radically new career—one where my schedule was fluid, I had expansive time to spend with my family, and I could spend my time helping women learn to find their own prosperity—I would have laughed in your face—and yet, here I was, and life was good.

All the stress, sleepless nights, worry, and soul searching I'd gone through to get here suddenly felt worth it, because they had gotten me here. And everything I was stepping into had started as a line item on my "prosperity list."

Still feeling a bit overwhelmed, I headed up the driveway and into the house. My prosperity was evident to me in every moment that evening. I had expansive time to prepare dinner with Jody, and afterwards, he, my son, and I sat on the porch after dinner, excited to talk about our days. Thanks to my careful budgeting and tracking, I wasn't worried about where the money for the mortgage would come from, or how I would afford both the cost of our new furniture *and* the vacation I was planning for us. And then, there was Jody: upbeat, social, kind, romantic, spiritual … the perfect partner with whom to share this new, prosperous, exciting, gratitude-filled life.

If I hadn't been standing right there in the middle of all of it, I would have pinched myself.

This happy ending was no accident. It happened because I set the stage for it through my LifeStyle Re-Design Planning process. I looked at all six Pillars of my life, and made the changes that were needed, even when they were hard—even when they challenged me to my core. I became the person I needed to be in order to live the life I wanted to live.

Today, I continue to engage in my own LifeStyle Re-Design Planning process even as I share it with my clients and students. Every month, I sit down and go over my six Pillars in detail, asking, "How can I be even more in alignment with my prosperity?" Sometimes, the answers surprise me—like when I was literally instructed in a meditation to write this book, even though I had no idea how I was going to do it!—but the guidance I get is always for my highest good.

YOUR RE-DESIGNED LIFE

When your six Pillars are in balance, and you start really making strides toward your prosperity through deliberate action, something magical happens. Things start to go your way. Opportunities open up. "Lucky breaks" abound. Why? It's the Law of Attraction at work. The more you set yourself up to attract—and sustain—the prosperity you desire, the more of that prosperity will come to you.

Here's a perfect example of how this can look. Dee called me a few months after I had moved into my new home. Nine months earlier, she had been literally sideswiped by her ex (who was also her business partner) when he not only dropped the divorce bomb but emptied their home of half their belongings in one weekend—*while Dee was away on a business trip!* She was left with no opportunity to talk things through or understand where this was coming from. In her desperation to save the marriage, she agreed to whatever he wanted, thinking that if she did, his mid-life crisis would grind to a halt and she could get her best friend and business partner back. Of course, that wasn't what happened, and she was left out in the cold to redesign not only her personal life, but her business life as well.

We did a lot of work around her Habits and Emotional Pillars, and helped her resolve some of the spending habits that were cropping up around the sudden sense of worthlessness and instability that had been triggered by her divorce. She was able to clearly see her life as it was, and make an empowered plan to rebuild. Nine months and one new business later, she decided to take a big leap into her new life.

"Michelle," she gushed, "I've made a big decision. I'm moving back to Manhattan! I'm not loving New Hampshire anymore—we only moved here because he wanted to—but I didn't have it in me to make any major changes until I started working with you. Doing this work has shown me that I can make it work no matter what, and I'm going for it!"

"That's amazing, Dee!" I told her.

"But that's not the best part! I told a few friends that I wanted to go back to the city, and one of them offered to sublet his apartment to me for six months for half the market value! It's right across from Central Park—pure heaven! Of course I said yes. I'm packing up the house today and I've signed a contract to put it on the market. The Realtor says she thinks she already has a perfect buyer, too!"

Boom! Do you see how that worked? Dee decided what she wanted, and went for it—and the moment she committed herself, amazing opportunities opened up for her.

When you apply and implement the LifeStyle Re-Design Planning process, your life won't be the same. You'll no longer be looking through filters of wishing and wondering and avoiding and playing small. You'll be taking your prosperity into your own hands, where you can shape it as you see fit. It's not always easy, especially at first, but it's always worth it. It's like designing a cool quilt, one square at a time; at first, all you can see is the mess of fabric scraps. But as you implement your plan, and start piecing things together, you'll soon see the shape of a life that's beautiful, unique, and totally focused on what's important to you.

Not everyone dreams of moving to Manhattan and living parkside. To some people, prosperity looks like knowing that, no matter what, you will have what you need. It's about being free from worry, and feeling like a creator in your life instead of a tag-along.

Rebecca was in awe when, after our first four sessions, her plan design was in place and ready to go. In just a few months, she was able to build an emergency fund and pay off the bulk of her non-mortgage debt. When she filed her tax return just after we finished our planning, she called me ecstatic. Because of the planning we'd done, she knew exactly where her $4,800 refund was going: to round out her emergency fund and pay off all of her remaining credit card bills. To her, this wasn't just the relief of getting out of debt; it was confirmation that, with good planning, she really could create the life she wanted.

Missy realized quickly that the control she'd gained through her LifeStyle Re-Design Planning flowed over into all areas of her life. When we worked on her plan, one of her goals was to incorporate healthier habits and make self-care a priority. She budgeted a CrossFit membership and extra money for fresh, organic food. After six months, she'd dropped forty-two pounds and was feeling stronger than she had in decades. She completed her first Spartan race, which proved to her that she truly could do anything she set her mind to. She attributed this directly to the work we had done in her Emotional and Habits Pillars, because they went so much deeper than financial finesse. "The best thing," she confided, "is that I'm not all 'doom and gloom' anymore. I have a new level of confidence, and I feel hopeful for the first time in a long time—maybe ever!"

Just like Dee, Rebecca, and Missy, this work will open new doors for you. You will start to see changes in your spending and saving patterns. You will form new habits. New doors will open. You will have a new sense of freedom and control, and feel like you can shape a whole new life for yourself at will.

Some of my clients tell me, "Things are so different now that I feel like I'm living someone else's life."

"But it's your life," I remind them. "The one that you decided you wanted, and that you took strategic steps to build. How does it feel?"

The answer is usually a single word: "Awesome!"

PUTTING IT ALL TOGETHER

If I'd had a roadmap to follow, or someone who could support me in this way during my own divorce, I would have saved myself a ton of time and several false starts. I would have set my GPS to "Prosperity After Divorce" and followed the navigation prompts to the letter. This book is your GPS—the special guidance system I've built to share with women who are ready to get in the driver's seat in their own lives and put the pedal to the metal.

I know this process works because I see the proof every day—in the spreadsheets in front of me, in the excited phone calls from clients, and in my own ever-growing prosperity and joy. I see amazing transformations happen all the time.

So many women come into my programs feeling broken. They are confused, uncertain, raw, and hurt. Some are walking in the shadow of their deepest fears, so frightened of what their future might hold that they can't move a muscle. Some are living in a state of scarcity even when, financially, they have more than enough. All arrive with a hope and desire to create something different for themselves, and birth the next chapter of their life in a more clear, empowered way.

With LifeStyle Re-Design Planning, everything becomes clearer. The fog starts to lift. This clarity is the reason why it works so well. Nothing is hidden anymore. I help clients allocate dollars and cents to various categories in their budget— and at the same time, reveal their true priorities and set them up to create positive progress that actually matters to them.

Right now is the time to create your plan and put it into play. You have done the hard work of peering into the darkest corners of your own emotions, habits, and finances, and you've gathered information about all six Pillars of your life— Financial, Emotional, Habits, Work, Family, and Spiritual. Now, it's time to put it all together into a cohesive plan to move you toward your vision for prosperity after divorce.

Your overall plan is going to follow this equation:

(Faith + Budget + Goals + Action)
+ (Habits + Emotions) =
YOUR PROSPERITY QUOTIENT

That looks complicated, but it's actually quite straightforward. Your belief, plus budget, plus your goals and the actions you take toward them, add up to your level of prosperity. Your habits and emotions can either add to or take away from that first number; even if you work hard, you can still undermine your prosperity if your emotions and habits are not in balance. This is why my LifeStyle Re-Design Planning process goes so much deeper than just creating a budget.

Your first step is to complete all of the action steps in this book (if you haven't already). Actually doing the exercises (as opposed to just thinking about them as you read) will give you the insight you need to put together a clear picture of your life, finances, priorities, emotions, habits, family dynamic, and belief systems, and allow you to start to plan for your future. Then, create your monthly budgets to reflect this plan, with your extra funds prioritized according to the 7 Baby Steps and your version of prosperity.* Every time you pay off a bill, put money in your emergency fund, or save enough for a trip or a well-deserved treat, you will feel yourself moving one step closer to true prosperity!

Big Goals, Small (and Temporary) Steps

When we started working together, Lexie was determined to get back on track. She wanted to go back to school and finish her nursing degree—but she was already working full-time *and* raising her two kids. She opted to reduce her work hours a bit and take on student loan debt in the short term to have what she really wanted in the long term.

While she was in school, she also opted to pare back a number of other expenses to minimize the impact of the new debt she was taking on. She eliminated her cable TV and premium channels subscriptions (keeping internet only), changed her cell phone plan, stopped getting her nails done, and cut eating out to a bare minimum. She also took a couponing class and was able to reduce her grocery bill by $30 per week.

Fast forward three years. Lexie is now in a comfortable, well-paying job made possible by her nursing degree. She has already eliminated most of her student loan debt, and has paid off the credit card bills she accumulated while in school. She has a retirement savings account and an emergency fund. She no longer worries about money on a daily basis. And all of this

---

*If you're struggling with this piece, you may need more support. Don't worry, I've got your back! On the Resources page, I share how you can work with me through my group and private coaching programs to get personalized support and create your Prosperity Plan with me.

is possible for her because she made strategic decisions based on her vision for prosperity and her long-term goals. More importantly, she was willing to sacrifice in the short term so she could have what she really wanted in the long term.

Anne and her ex never had any common interests beyond their kids. Anne had always wanted to travel to new places; he wanted to visit the same town, year after year. Not once had they taken a trip to see their grown children, who both lived in different time zones with their own families; he said they were living their own lives, and could come back to visit. They were both at the end of their careers, and neither had done anything exciting or unusual. When she talked to her husband about this, he shut her down, saying, "Stop watching the Travel Channel. Those dreams just aren't in the cards."

The thing was, money wasn't tight. They had always had more than enough, but Anne's husband controlled the budget so tightly that even the occasional splurge was out of the question.

Anne pleaded for marriage counseling. He said nothing was wrong. She just had to stop wanting another life. Finally, after thirty-nine years, she decided that she wasn't willing to sacrifice her dreams any longer. She *did* want another life, and not with him.

Fourteen months after she asked for a divorce, Anne and I sat together for a private VIP day to work on her LifeStyle Re-Design Plan. It was clear that she wanted to have the freedom to travel to see her kids, especially since twin grand-children were on their way in the very near future! Prosperity, to Anne, meant the freedom to choose how, when, and where she would enjoy the fruits of her labor. She named her vacation envelope "FREEDOM!"

She couldn't have it all at once, since she was now living on one income, but we created a plan that would incorporate her goals and dreams. As we worked out the details, it was clear that she was willing to sacrifice things like eating out (which most of her single friends were doing) and instead create a weekly meal plan to avoid overspending. Her children had given her a NetFlix subscription and an Amazon FireStick for her birthday, so she didn't need a cable TV subscription; instead, she planned to reallocate what she would have spent on that to her FREEDOM envelope. Everywhere we found a place where Anne could save money, she committed to adding that cash to her travel fund. Three months later, she was on a plane for the first time in her life, heading to the left coast to see her new grandbabies.

****

When I sold my business, I had to take on a number of additional expenses that I wasn't used to absorbing. One was the cost of my car. Before, I'd always had a company car. Yes, I paid for it because I owned the company, but it wasn't tallied every month in my personal budget. Now, I had to factor in not only a car payment, but also insurance, gas, and taxes.

To offset this, I got rid of the luxury car I'd been driving and bought a hybrid. This would save me $100 or more a month in gas, and my insurance, taxes, and repair costs would be cut in half. Now, I won't lie: going from a top-level Acura Sport to a Ford Fusion took a bit of getting used to, but instead of having a pity party over it, I reminded myself why I was doing it. I wanted real prosperity, not just a bunch of money and stuff. My short-term enjoyment in the driver's seat was worth sacrificing to get what I really wanted in the long run.

Back in the introduction to Part II, we talked about setting your big goals for prosperity after divorce. What did you paint on your life canvas? Where do you see yourself in three years? Five? Ten?

Now, ask yourself the following question: *"What am I willing to sacrifice right now so that I can have what I really want in the long term?"*

Be ruthless with this. Is your cable TV subscription more important to you than your emergency fund? Is your daily latte habit more important to you than world travel? These aren't silly questions. If you keep doing things the way you've always done them—and you don't have an unlimited supply of money—these are the tradeoffs you will make. Most people never get ahead because they aren't willing to sacrifice the little rewards for the big picture payoff.

Revisit the work you did in the introduction to Part II to identify your goals. Then, look at the work you've done in the six Pillars, especially your monthly budget line items. What can be changed or eliminated in the short term to help you meet your goals?

Remember, you don't have to make these changes permanently—only for long enough to change your financial situation and get to where you want to be. If you really want to pick up that latte habit again in three years, you can totally do it—but chances are, you won't.

COMMON ROADBLOCKS

Even with the best GPS, you can still run into roadblocks and diversions. Sometimes, you don't know something will be a problem until it happens. But a slowdown or even a closed road isn't a reason to give up on your LifeStyle Re-Design Plan.

Some of the common roadblocks you may hit include:

- *Having to play catch-up on overdue bills.* (Note: this is *not* a reason not to do this work. In fact, it's an even bigger reason to do this work, and actually devise a plan!)

- *An emergency arises before you have your Emergency Fund fully established*, and you're suddenly back to square one.

- *An expense arises in a planned category* (such as auto repairs), but shows up before you have been able to accumulate enough of a cushion in that envelope to cover the expense.

- *You lose your job* (or your income fluctuates seasonally).

- *Your child support or alimony income is not received per the divorce agreement*, or is received late.

- *You have additional legal expenses* due to post-divorce issues (such as the late/unpaid child support described above).

- *Emotions get the best of you and you go on a spending spree.*

- *You've lost your spiritual anchor* and don't believe that the future can (and will) get better for you.

- *You struggle with personal accountability,* goal setting, and discipline.

We can't do it all, all the time. We all need support, and a support system is an integral part of long-term success. Asking for help is a strength, not a weakness—and seeking the help you need is the best gift you can give yourself as you create your prosperity. The key is to keep your eyes and heart open enough to recognize when you've hit a roadblock or gotten lost and need someone to guide you back to a place where you can find your way again.

Many women come to me because they're seeking more help than what they are getting from their families, friends, therapists, or divorce teams. They come seeking a roadmap, of course—but also the strategies and skills to get themselves back on track when they hit those rough spots. They want to learn, grow, and walk insightfully as they regain their financial footing.

As I tell those clients, dealing with roadblocks is about more than making the numbers work. It's about owning your power—your internal fortitude, resolution, and unshakable belief that you are capable and skilled enough to create your vision of prosperity after divorce. Before we can create prosperity, we need to find that belief inside ourselves. Once we have it, it will propel us, support us, and nourish us, no matter what. It doesn't matter how much money you have: if you don't feel in control and empowered in your own life and choices (financial and otherwise), you will never feel secure. When those roadblocks arise (which they inevitably will) you won't deal with them in a clear, decisive way that will get you back on track and moving in the right direction. Instead, you'll flounder, spin your wheels, or get yourself so lost and disoriented that you won't know which way is up.

Leesa was divorcing her psychotherapist husband after eight years of marriage. Thanks to a multi-million-dollar inheritance from her mother, who had passed the year before, and an existing relationship with a notable wealth management firm, Leesa was in great shape financially. But she didn't feel secure inside—which was why she came to me.

Leesa's husband had been verbally abusive to both her and her daughter for years. He was extremely manipulative and condescending, and the constant barrage of cruelty and insults ate away at her confidence. Now that they were in mediation, she was reaching out to me for guidance about establishing a solid footing for herself, and making empowered choices during the mediation, which was still in process.

Leesa was not my first client with substantial wealth. Her LifeStyle Re-Design plan was not going to be about monthly budgeting and debt repayment as much as it was about making good financial decisions to preserve and grow what she already had. She also needed someone to discuss decisions with in the moment, so she didn't cave to her ex's pressure and narcissistic demands.

The day she called me, she had just left a mediation session. They had agreed to sell the marital home, but had been arguing for two months about who the realtor should be, and what the listing price would look like. Leesa knew that even if she could get him to come to an agreement, he would probably reject any offer "on principle." But today, something unexpected had happened. Her ex had told her to "Just keep the house. It's not going to be worth much once the mortgage is paid off anyway." Of course, this was music to her ears—*if* he actually agreed to it on paper. But it also brought up a whole slew of questions. What kind of new home could she actually afford? What if she found her new home before the old one sold? Could she manage both on her fixed dividend income? If not, what should she ask for in mediation to ensure that she didn't blow through a ton of money while she waited for the market to be on her side?

She needed a detailed roadmap and action steps to approach this with confidence. We walked through all of the steps, and all of the worst-case scenarios. Afterward, Leesa was already feeling more confident and empowered. In her next mediation session, she spoke up for what she actually wanted and needed, instead of simply responding to her ex's tirades.

Here is what she sent me after she sold her marital home and closed on her new one—all in the same week!

> *Michelle, you have a delightful mix of financial savvy and intuitive wisdom. Working with you has deepened my appreciation for the resources available to support me on my prosperity journey, which is particularly helpful after a painful divorce. Your warmth, enthusiasm, and devotion to empowering women is a gift, and one I would strongly encourage any woman to consider. What could be a greater gift than an ongoing cultivation and deepening of our highest expression of abundance on every level? Thank you so much for walking with me!*

My heart swells when I see women move from uncertainty and paralysis to a more focused outlook. They gain control— and as they do, they gain confidence. It's like riding a bike with training wheels; after a little while, you can feel that you now have the courage and stamina to pedal on your own, even when you hit a bump.

Roadblocks will happen. So, instead of letting them derail your prosperity, use them as learning opportunities to show you where you can find extra support and assistance.

If you feel stuck, you can:

- Find an accountability partner.

- Join my Prosperity After Divorce Private Support Group on Facebook.

- Sign up for an online workshop or course.

- Reach out for private help if you need it.

No matter what the situation, when a roadblock hits, it's time to go back to the drawing board. Go over your budget, income, expenses, and projections. What needs to shift to get you back on track with key items like your emergency fund or retirement savings? What short-term changes can you make to recoup some extra money every month? What are you willing to do in the short term to reach your long-term prosperity goals?

KEEP GOING!

When we want lasting change, we need to take a slow-but-steady approach.

My longtime friend Cathy Frost teaches this so well in her work, "Forget Diets Forever." When we do the latest fad or crash diet, we may lose weight quickly—but we soon start to struggle with keeping the weight off, or sticking to an unrealistic diet plan. On the other hand, taking a holistic, lifestyle-based approach to our wellness and shedding just a few pounds a month provides a much more sustainable long-term result.

It's the same with approaching your LifeStyle Re-Design Planning. When I introduce this work to women, I emphasize the slow and steady implementation and learning. Many women who attend a workshop or listen in on a webinar leave expecting to implement everything over the next few days, but the results are equivalent to a crash diet—scattered and mediocre. You can't expect to change your whole life in three hours and make it stick.

So, let me ask you: Did you pick up this book to create mediocre short-term gains or lasting prosperity? I'm guessing it's the latter—and if so, cut yourself some slack!

Long-lasting, positive change comes from the ability to digest and embrace each Pillar of our lives—to master each task, and make it your own. When you do this, you will eventually wake up and find that what was foreign and scary to you is now normal and exciting. That's exactly what happens to my clients over and over again, and it's awesome to watch.

With this long-term implementation plan in mind, revisit your LifeStyle Re-Design Planning process every six months. This will help you stay on track, see clearly where you have slipped back into old habits, and—most importantly—give you a clear view of how far you've come.

Celebrating your wins is a big part of this process. Sometimes, especially when we have to make big changes to our habits and emotional patterns, the first couple of months of sticking to a budget can test us. Reviewing our goals and looking at the progress we've made is the best way to show our minds and hearts that we are on the right track.

As you move further toward your prosperity goals, you will probably notice that you have slightly more disposable income. When your planning has empowered you to pay off debt, start an emergency fund, and indulge in a vacation or two, you may be tempted to start slipping back into old, habitual spending patterns, simply because you can. Why not eat out five days a week? You have the money now. Why not go on a shopping spree? It won't break the bank. Of course you should indulge yourself once in a while—but you should only allow yourself to change a habit when it fits in with your greater plan.

Every six months, create a new goals sheet, review and tweak your budget in areas that need it (remember, you are budgeting each and every month), and a new plan. Go through the six Pillars and track your spending, habits, and action steps in each. Get out your bank statements and your calculator and get the big picture of your life. Then, make the adjustments that are necessary to keep going toward (or realign yourself with) your vision for prosperity. The more consistently you do this, the faster you will create the life you really want.

The Bottom Line

This is your life. Yours. No one else's.

No one can tell you what prosperity looks like for you—not even me. Your vision is unique—but no matter what your vision looks like, and no matter where you're starting from, the LifeStyle Re-Design Planning process can get you there.

If everyone were living according to their goals, dreams, and visions, the world would be a better place, don't you think?

That's why it's my dream for you to create a life that makes you feel happy, joyful, loved, valued, fulfilled, empowered, and excited. When you create your vision of prosperity, the echoes of that positivity ripple throughout your whole life, and touch all the people in it.

With love, abundance, and unshakable faith in your prosperous future,

Michelle

Part IV

WORKSHEETS

Use these worksheets to help you get
even more out of the exercises I've
described in the chapters.

MY NEEDS AND WANTS

Leaving the numbers out of the equation, spend some time working through what you need versus what you want. Your LifeStyle Re-Design Planning process will help you attain your wants without sacrificing your needs!

Needs	*Wants*

MY PROSPERITY VISION

The vision I have for myself and my life is ...

_____

_____

_____

_____

_____

_____

_____

_____

_____

_____

_____

_____

_____

_____

_____

_____

_____

HOME INVENTORY CHECKLIST (Make one copy for each room in your home)

Item	Description	Qty	Purchased during marriage?	Approx. current value	Who is keeping? (If unsure, mark as "dispute")	Approx. cost to replace?
				$		$
				$		$
				$		$
				$		$
				$		$
				$		$
				$		$
				$		$
				$		$
				$		$
				$		$
				$		$
				$		$
				$		$
				$		$
				$		$

LIFESTYLE RE-DESIGN PLANNING
SIMPLE BUDGET WORKSHEET

Using the information you gathered in Chapter Five, fill in each of the line items on this spreadsheet.

TOTAL MONTHLY INCOME from all sources (paychecks, support, interest, bonuses, other)	$

Housing expenses	$
Debt repayments	$
Seasonal Purchases	$
Transportation expenses	$
Food & household items	$
Clothing & accessories	$
Medical, dental, vision & health	$
Personal expenses	$
Kids' expenses	$
Travel	$
Pets	$
Gifts & charity	$
Miscellaneous	$
Savings	$
Other	$
TOTAL MONTHLY EXPENSES from all sources	$

EMOTIONAL SPENDING WORKSHEET

Review the last 30-60 days of your purchases to ferret out
your emotional spending habits (refer to the Common Emotional
Spending Triggers section in Chapter Six) and match each purchase
with its emotional trigger.

Emotional Purchase	Reason/Trigger ?

HABITS PILLAR CHECKLIST (Cost analysis for habitual spending)

Habit (Ex: Daily Latte Stop)	Daily cost	Monthly cost	Yearly cost	Alternative option(s)	Alternate cost/ annual savings
	$	$	$		$
	$	$	$		$
	$	$	$		$
	$	$	$		$
	$	$	$		$
	$	$	$		$
	$	$	$		$
	$	$	$		$
	$	$	$		$
	$	$	$		$
	$	$	$		$
	$	$	$		$
	$	$	$		$
	$	$	$		$
TOTALS	$	$	$		$

Extras

Acknowledgments

My deepest, heartfelt gratitude goes out to …

Every woman who has been through a divorce and invited me onto their path. The journey with each of you has been heart driven, purposeful and down right fabulous. Thank you for letting me be part of your tribe and for trusting me not only with your dollars and cents, but with your grief, your hopes, and—most importantly—your prosperity dreams.

My own supportive tribe: Rosemarie, my mother, friend, and biggest cheerleader, who has been not only my rock, but my inspiration and example to become the best mother I can be. My children, for embracing and rising through the storms not of your choosing, and for trusting me when all I could muster was a promise to provide you a safe and loving home (even though you deserved that plus the sun, the stars and the moon).

Kristie, Andrea, Kristen, Veronica, Anita, Kimberly, Donna W., Sharon, Laura, Sue—my lifelong girlfriends and "Boo-Hoo" crew: Thank you for always surfing the waves of life with me, and for taking time to enjoy the ride with me! The strength I draw from your friendships, love, and support is immeasurable, and your ability to come bearing wine, tissues, and chocolate when needed is lifesaving.

Bryna Haynes, my editor and creative partner in crime for taking this project on at thirty-nine weeks pregnant! Thank you for seeing the value of my work, and for your willingness to work during the wee hours of the night over these past few months, while everyone else was sleeping, to make my project come to life. You are a rockstar!

Jeff, My pastor and Carol, his wife, for being incredible guides to me while I was working in my own Spiritual Pillar. I'm so grateful for your insights, wisdom, and encouragement to stay the course when my inner critic cried foul around this purpose-driven work. The delivery of those divine downloads arrived just when I needed them!

And lastly, to my husband Jody. You are a constant reminder that dreams do come true. You have continually walked with me, allowed my prosperity journey to unfold alongside of yours, and encouraged me with love and appreciation. You helped heal my broken heart, and I'm forever grateful for your desire and commitment to love me just as I am.

MICHELLE JACOBIK

Do you want more support in your prosperity journey?
You're in the right place!

• *Live Events* •

• *Virtual Group Coaching* •

• *Money Day Spa programs* •

• *One-on-one coaching* •
& financial analysis

—— visit ——

MICHELLEJACOBIK.COM

to access my event calendar, learn more about my coaching services, and
download free resources like my payment calculators, e-books, and more!

About the Author

An expert in money, business, and finance, Michelle Jacobik is a highly sought-after budget coach. Her Financial Solutions and Divorce Support Programs have successfully led individuals around the country in rebuilding their financial foundations. Using her trademarked LifeStyle Re-Design Planning™ process, she incorporates budgeting tools, debt reduction planning, and saving techniques with a sprinkle of discovery coaching to help clients forge their way towards their prosperity goals. She is a contributing writer for *Thrive Global* and *DivorceForce Magazine,* among others, and brings her message of hope and prosperity as a guest on local and national podcasts and radio shows. Her previous books, *5 Things You Must Know Before Signing a Settlement* and *The 5 Key Ingredients to Building Financial Freedom,* were published in 2015 and 2016.

Through her live events, small group online workshops, and one-on-one private sessions, Michelle has helped thousands of women define and connect with their vision for a fulfilling life after divorce and become their most courageous selves through targeted financial action. Her programs provide a roadmap that allows women to hone their financial savvy while creating a life of joy, freedom, purpose—and, of course, prosperity.

After more than fifteen years as a veteran business owner and sales leader providing conscientious and realistic insurance protection strategies to corporate clients, and with twenty-eight years of experience in insurance and financial services to her credit, Michelle redirected her core values and leadership skills to provide "one on one"and B2B Financial Coaching. Her diverse background includes expertise in tax preparation as well as life and estate planning solutions. She held her Securities license from 1989-2011, is a Dave Ramsey Trained Independent Financial Counselor, holds a Professional Coaching Certification through the International Coach Certification Academy, and is a Certified Divorce Financial Analyst (CDFA) through the Institute for Divorce Analysts.

Michelle lives in Connecticut with her husband Jody, where they have created their own version of prosperity after divorce on ten beautiful acres of farmland with their blended family of seven, a crazy cat named Bella, and a rescue dog named Duncan. Michelle loves good food, wine, and chocolate (not necessarily in that order) and will travel anywhere she can plant her feet in warm sand and soak up the sun alongside her mom, Rosemarie.

To learn more about Michelle, visit MichelleJacobik.com.